Caleb

An Ordinary Man
A Courageous Journey

Ingrid Dacker

Caleb: An Ordinary Man, A Courageous Journey
Written and illustrated by Ingrid Dacker

Copyright © 2023 by Ingrid Dacker.

All rights reserved. Apart from any fair dealing for the purpose of study, research, criticism, or review, as permitted under the copyright act, no part may be reproduced by any means without written
permission.
www.ingriddacker.com

Cover illustration: Copyright © 2023 by Ingrid Dacker. All rights reserved.
Cover design: Lisa Schroder

Edited by Helga Hooley and Lexia G Mackin

Caleb is based on real events and real characters. Some events have been fictionalized. Names have been changed for privacy.

ISBN: 978-0-6458001-1-1 Paperback
ISBN: 978-0-6458001-1-1 eBook

For my family.

With special thanks to
my husband, Garry
Ann, Karl, Helga, Lexia and Lisa.

This book would not be if not for your help.

Table of Contents

Prologue	2
Chapter One	7
Chapter Two	21
Chapter Three	27
Chapter Four	31
Chapter Five	39
Chapter Six	43
Chapter Seven	51
Chapter Eight	55
Chapter Nine	67
Chapter Ten	77
Chapter Eleven	83
Chapter Twelve	97
Chapter Thirteen	105
Chapter Fourteen	115
Chapter Fifteen	131
Chapter Sixteen	139
Chapter Seventeen	149
Chapter Eighteen	165
Chapter Nineteen	175
Chapter Twenty	183
Chapter Twenty One	191
Epilogue	197
Glossary	199

Prologue

A flickering streetlamp cast murky shadows that played my mind like a cat and mouse, its intermittent light revealing the indistinct outline of deserted storefronts, the dingy remnants of what had once been. Clouds obscured the moon and tendrils of mist curled their way through the abandoned street.

It felt like the hair-trigger tension in the moments before a shoot-out in an old Western. All my senses stood at full attention: scanning, peering, listening. A movie would have had suitably mysterious, dramatic music but this was no movie. Whether it was a dream, a trance or a vision I couldn't tell you, but I knew it was real, very real.

Where am I? What is this place? Nothing felt familiar. I could feel the hairs on the back of my neck stand on end.

A man was standing beside me!

"Whaa!"

I jumped backwards, facing him, adrenaline coursing through me.

"Who are you?" The hoarse question erupted from my parched throat.

CALEB

"I am the Restorer." The quiet words hung in the air.

Restorer! What? Who? What sort of name is that? Where did he spring from?

I glared at him through the semi-darkness, trying to take his measure, my heart pounding against my chest, my mind racing. He seemed familiar somehow, but I couldn't place him. Had I met him before? I didn't know. He didn't look like a threat but…

Get a grip, Caleb, I told myself, trying to gain some equilibrium.

He was unremarkable, the sort of person you could pass in the street and not really notice. Of medium build with dark curves of hair and casual beard, he was dressed in jeans and T-shirt. He was maybe in his early thirties from what I could make out in the poor light. Like I said, he was unremarkable, except for his eyes. It was his eyes that caught my attention, deep pools of stillness that seemed to radiate. What was it about his eyes? They were completely riveting, unfazed by my scrutiny. Without him saying a word they were calming me.

They were what kept me there, rooted to the spot, instead of following my instinct and making tracks out of that freaky place.

He drew my attention to one of the dilapidated buildings.

The moon escaped the clouds and swirling mist to allow me to make out a dark and foreboding structure. It looked like something in grey scale or an eerie scene from a fairy tale and gave no indication of life. It may once have been an old service station, a warehouse, or a workshop. The gloom hid any signage that would have given any clue as to its identity. The vacant block next door was like a tip, the discarded accumulation of junk covered with weeds. Every door and window in the building was boarded up. The message was 'KEEP OUT!' in no uncertain terms. Vines had taken possession of every surface as if to reinforce the stance. It was not a welcoming sight. An involuntary shudder danced down my spine.

Derelict place like that just needs bulldozing I reckon. What is this place anyway? I mused, scanning the depressing sight.

My internal pondering was interrupted as the man answered my thoughts. "This is your life," He said calmly.

"Wh-What did you just say!?" My voice betrayed me, sounding disembodied and hoarse.

My life? If someone had asked me how I was, I would have told them I was fine. I would have believed it—totally—at least throughout the day. I was a bit tired and grumpy maybe, but I was completely fine.

During the day I kept busy, distracted by a mess of plans and decisions and responsibilities, doggedly determined to push through. Anything negative was neatly packed away out of sight, out of mind.

Nights were another matter altogether. They were spent tossing and turning, a jumble of thoughts stole sleep with their accusations, like a pack of wolves, circling, enjoying the anticipation, smelling the blood.

At night it felt like there was nothing left of my life but the flotsam of abandoned failures and aborted dreams. Despair haunted the hours of darkness.

My latest ventures were not going well. I had bought into an end of day trading system and completed courses to learn to read charts to indicate when to buy and sell shares. The broker they provided was supposed to be there for support and assistance.

My wife, Sarah, had been fine with me doing the course and taking the leap. In fact, she had encouraged me.

The little share trading scheme had started well. I had done some good trades, made some decent money but not lately. Now I was chasing losses. I had thought I could make up for the last bad trade, but I had really made a hash of it this time. I had gone along with what my broker suggested; not for the first time either. *Why? What could I have been thinking?*

There is a good reason why those blokes are called brokers. Mind you, I

CALEB

could think of a lot of other names for them too; none of them very nice. I didn't even think it through properly. It wasn't rational! It was as if I had lost my mojo altogether. I had probably broken every rule I had been taught.

How much was I down? I didn't know for sure—I wasn't game to work it out. It was part of the great avoidance.

I hadn't told Sarah either, not yet. Lately I had stopped telling my wife lots of things. I didn't think the marriage would survive another blow. That's what I told myself anyway.

Man! This time it was a lot of money. Damn it! How did I do that? Why? What was I thinking, grabbing at some vain hope, some futile life raft?

You #$%@# SUCKER Peter Browne! I derided myself angrily. God, what a mess! I had thought that I could make a bit of extra money, support the family while we renovated the house we had bought. Yeah sure! Great plan! But everything was turning pear-shaped. Was I just following the crowd? Was I afraid of missing out? I had no idea. I blamed my broker—a lot—but I mostly blamed myself.

Then there was the renovation, a BIG renovation.

Why? What was in my head?

We had sold the house we had previously modernized for a tidy profit and wanted to go again. We could hardly be considered 'flippers', like the TV big shots, but I liked the idea of increasing equity with a bit of hard work and creativity. Sarah had suggested we downsize and buy an investment property as well as one for ourselves, but the very thought of living cramped up in suburbia made me feel claustrophobic. My total lack of enthusiasm for any of her suggestions finally wore her down and we began to look at houses on larger blocks. They were as rare as hen's teeth, especially within 'cooee' of town. After months of searching, we found one in a perfect location only 10 minutes from town on about 2.7 hectares. It was a big rambling house built in the early 80's but required much more work than I had planned to take on.

This renovation was nowhere near as easy as the last one. Everything seemed to be hard— overwhelmingly, frustratingly hard. I felt completely out of my depth.

After weeks of flogging myself, night after night, a memory from childhood had unexpectedly intruded into the turmoil of thoughts in the predawn darkness.

It was dark and way past my bedtime. Dad had been looking after my sister  and me while Mum enjoyed an evening out with a friend at a special ladies' event. Her friend's husband had picked Mum up, delivered them both to the venue, and gone off fishing. Now it was Dad's turn to pick them both up. Mum never learnt to drive so she relied on others if she needed to go anywhere, not uncommon for women of her era.

I knew it! I knew what was going to happen and I knew my Dad wouldn't want me to come. I was supposed to be asleep like my younger sister. This whole untenable arrangement depended on it. Dad couldn't manage the two of us in the front of the Austin A40 ute on his own. I didn't have a clue about that. I just knew that I didn't want to miss out on a ride in the car. No way! But most of all I was terrified at the thought of being left on my own.

"I want to go with you Dad!"

"Go to sleep Caleb."

"I want to come. I don't want you to leave me behind!" Silence was the only response.

"I'm going with you Dad." I was desperate and determined.

"I WANT TO GO WITH YOU, DAD!"

"Dad, Dad, Dad!" But he pulled away. I couldn't stop him pulling away from me.

My distressed vigilance continued with practiced persistence for a long time until finally fussing subsided into exhausted sleep. The tactic always worked on Mum but with Dad it was like frantically trying to grab hold of smoke, curling through my fingers, and gone; something that was determined to get away—inanimate and distant but with determination as cold as steel.

I finally drifted off only to startle awake with the realization that he was gone. Dread mingled with anger. He went! He waited until I settled down and then he went. Rage joined the desperation in protest at the helplessness of the situation. I felt so very little and alone.

Mum never ventured out on her own again while we were little.

∾

The memory had sprung from a hidden vault of childhood but the feelings that dogged it were as close and familiar as the feel of the pillow on my face, saturated with the night's battle.

Dad, will I ever be good enough for you to notice me? Will I ever matter to you?

I had blamed my sister then. She was such a baby, two years younger than my 5 years, sleeping through the whole 'kerfuffle'. I was sure that it was her fault. I had no clue why.

Why does this keep happening to me? Why? A germ of realization was beginning to form in the wake of the unbidden memory as I wrestled for the strength to face the day. Could it be significant? It happened so long ago. I was just a kid. How could that affect me now?

"God help me. Please help me?" Desperation fuelled the question thrown into the air, without much hope of any response. *Why would He want to help me? Would He even hear, or care?*

Immediately the vision had begun as if in answer.

Chapter One

This place is my life!

Hang on! I hadn't said anything out loud! Did this dude just read my thoughts? This is weird!

I stared balefully at the man beside me.

"What, that building? It's my life?!" There was accusation in my questions.

"Ah-huh." He nodded.

I'm usually a very calm, logical sort of bloke. I don't rattle easily but this was a serious head-spin. I'm sure I didn't say anything out loud.

Nah, I'm just dreaming, I argued with myself.

What's he on about? This is me? No, nuh, it can't be!

Dear Lord, what have I got myself into? What is this? What's happening? I shook my head, my mind groped for understanding. Conflicting thoughts collided in my mind in a flurry of confusion, vying for attention, scattering my emotions in every direction, like panicked birds.

For the second time in a few moments, I shuddered. What is he on about?

CALEB

It's got to be some sort of bad dream. I could feel adrenaline coursing, muscles tensing for escape.

He was completely unfazed by my hostility and abruptness.

"Shall we go in?"

He wants me to go in! In there? This was everything you tell your children not to do.

Get a grip man! I derided myself as I scrambled to regain some equilibrium. I slammed the door on the bird cage, bringing my emotions to heel.

I searched again for any signs of life, peering around towards the back, through the jungle of vegetation. There seemed to be a faint light coming from the back of the building. Could there be someone in there after all?

As I stood in front of the dark ominous building, I knew I was being faced with a choice. Don't ask me how. I just knew.

Facing the chaos of my life was about as appealing as dancing through a mine field! Is that what he means? Most of it I didn't even look at myself, let alone…

Really?

What was that going to unearth? A sort of cold terror resurfaced briefly before being shoved back down somewhere deep inside. I shook my head, trying to clear my thoughts.

But then, what did I have to lose? It could be thousands of dollars, my marriage, my kids or even the house. Yeh, maybe, if I keep going like this. As I silently wrestled to control the little birds in my brain, I became aware of the man beside me, patiently waiting for my response. Again, his eyes arrested me.

He had said "Shall *we* go in". I think he intends to come with me! I don't know why that thought made it feel less daunting, but somehow it did.

What would I be getting myself into? I stared at him blankly as I derided myself for even considering the suggestion but somehow, I was. I think I need to go in there! To somehow face—myself—seriously…

He waited in silence, allowing me time to consider.

"Okay". It was little more than a whisper.

"Okay. Let's do it," I said, more strongly this time. I had made my choice.

His response was immediate. He grinned at me and then turned his attention to the building. Dear God, he looks like he is going to enjoy this!

The tangled vines gave him no pause. He swept his hand in their direction and in a moment, they disappeared, taking the timber barricades with them. Wow! He made that look so easy. How did he do that? I was flabbergasted, the sense of unreality intensifying. He was enjoying this! And that wasn't all.

Happy Days! Everything was changing! Bright, shiny, corrugated iron now clad the once dingy street front. The whole street was coming alive, every building restored. It wasn't night-time anymore. It had changed from night to day with the wave of his hand, leaving my head spinning. How did that happen? The street, so recently deserted, started to teem with life, people walking their dogs, birds singing, cars whizzing past.

It took me a moment to realize that the cars were models from a bygone era. A 1960's Chevrolet convertible pranced past, driven by a young woman. She sported enormous sunglasses, and a beehive hair-do covered with a garish, patterned scarf. A shiny new two-tone EH Holden headed in the opposite direction. This was a complete freak out! Like a sci-fi movie or children's animation, only with real people. Maybe I was hallucinating?

The vacant block was still just as overgrown and uninviting. Darkness still shrouded the back of the vast building with only the faintest glimmer of light to give any relief but out on the street the transformation was amazing! Something was also happening inside me. I could feel hope beginning to surface.

The contrast was so stark it was almost ridiculous. The thought tickled me as I took in the scene unfolding in front of me. *It's as different as night and day*, I mused and was rewarded by a low chuckle from the man beside me. "Yep! It sure is," He responded to my thoughts.

I was caught off guard again. How in the whole world does he do that? I don't know if I could ever get used to that little trick. It was unsettling and totally unexpected to have him respond to my thoughts but still—comforting somehow. It surprised me that it felt safe and warm to have him share my amusement.

This man could charm the birds out of the trees—or maybe I was out of my tree? Who knows? I simply could not process all that was happening.

I shook my head again to clear it and took a deep breath. "Okay," I said, "I think I'm ready."

I pushed open a small side door and stepped inside. I took a moment for my eyes to adjust. The only light came from a grimy window set high in the wall and one lone, inadequate light bulb, festooned in decades of cobwebs. Discarded tools and miscellaneous bits and pieces were overshadowed by gloom and semidarkness. Very little of the bright sunlight that had suddenly appeared outside could penetrate. Dust motes danced their freedom in a narrow shaft of light as we walked, released from the thick layer of grime that obscured any logic that may have existed in the disarray.

"What a lot of garbage. It would take a bit to clear all this out," I said dryly, trying to take it all in. Thoughts of bulldozers and demolition resurfaced.

"No, it's not garbage. Sure, some of it needs to go, but lots of this has great value. It just needs a bit of a clean-up and some order restored in here," he said.

I did not share his perspective, or his confidence. It seemed like an impossible task and hardly worth the effort. It was a huge mess. Was he serious? How would you ever get this lot cleared out? It would take a lifetime sorting through it all.

We moved further inside. Sounds of pure frustration drifted towards us from somewhere down the back of the cavernous workshop. Whoa, there was someone in here after all and he sounded none too happy. Thoughts of high tailing it out of there surfaced again.

Memories came flooding back and I knew they were somehow connected to the scene unfolding in front of me. I remembered…

I had been hanging out at a mate's place when three of his cousins had rocked up, completely spoiling my plans for the afternoon. Why did a bunch of girls need to be here anyway? The sounds of the latest Beatles hit blaring from the stereo did little to cover my embarrassment.

I never did feel like I fitted in anywhere. I was painfully shy and awkward. I never gave much thought to my clothes but somehow, I knew that the blue plaid shirt my mum had bought for me didn't really look the part. Any sort of social event caused acute discomfort and as for talking to girls— They may as well have been a different species, maybe from a different planet. No, not Venus either, it's definitely not far enough away. I had no clue how to talk to them. Going to a boys' high school, one of the few public schools in Sydney not already integrated, probably didn't help that either. The place felt like it was full of complete strangers, most of them girls. I didn't really try to talk to any of them; I just mumbled something incoherent in reply if I found it unavoidable while carefully inspecting my shoes. If I did venture to say anything it was usually with my foot firmly planted in my mouth. I was okay with my mates. That was different. We could talk for hours, but this 'We gotta get out of this place if it's the last thing we ever do!' played again for at least the third time. Someone must really like that song! Eric Burdon and the Animals sang the now familiar words, expressing what I was screaming on the inside. 'Daddy, he's been working and slaving his life away—' Yep, they pretty much nailed it.

It wasn't just the impromptu party; I felt desperate to get away from the farm where I had grown up. The thousands of chooks and the dust they created played havoc with the asthma that plagued me. I knew I wasn't old enough yet but one day…

I wish I had come from a different family. Maybe then I would fit in. Could I just disappear right about now? Like, could the ground just open up or something? I wish I had never come here.

It didn't take long before I muttered my goodbyes and walked home.

Another memory encroached, feelings of shame and embarrassment riding its coat tails.

I had been to the city to my asthma specialist. It was quite a trip as a teenager, catching buses on my own. Now I was sitting waiting at the terminus for Dad with streams of people milling around.

Dad was a full-time primary producer. I mean full-time, seven days a week, dawn 'til after dark, 365 days a year! That's how it felt anyway. It always felt like it was an imposition for him to stop what he was doing to pick me up. I was stopping him from doing something important. I was never important— he always seemed so reluctant.

"Dad, would you hurry up? Please come and pick me up. Like, *now* would be good! For goodness' sake, where is he?"

"DAD! Where are you!!!"

When he finally did come, I felt ashamed of him in his ute, looking a mess in his old work clothes. I didn't want to be associated with him. *Dad, couldn't you have cleaned up a little bit? You knew you would be picking me up. What will others think? Everybody will see you*

I forced the memories aside. I became aware again of the man beside me and I glanced across at him. I felt none of the discomfort I usually felt with someone I had recently met despite the complete emotional upheaval of the last 20 minutes. I wonder why? My reactions had not exactly been—well—shall we say, friendly. It didn't seem to faze him.

We picked our way through the vast building, stopping now and then to dust off a discarded object. It felt so normal, so peaceful and yet so new to me.

He seemed so easy to just be with. I didn't have to make conversation, something I was never all that good at, especially with strangers. I could just *be*. He seemed to *get* me somehow, like nobody I had ever met. It struck me how unusual it was for me to feel so comfortable with someone I had just met.

As I looked at him the realization dawned on me that those guys back years ago at my mate's place and the milling crowds that had caused so much discomfort, they didn't care! It didn't matter to them what I looked like. All of that was in my head. Nobody else would have known what was going on inside me! I had fought so hard not to be the odd one out, all the time tormented, imagining what people would think. They didn't think anything, except maybe about themselves.

All of a sudden, I saw my Dad in a very different light too. Nobody cared what he looked like either! He was a hard-working farmer who had a lot to do— simple as that— and he took time out to pick me up. I had no clue where these new thoughts had come from, but they were freeing. It was as if a load had fallen off my shoulders. The relief was as profound as it was unexpected.

In some extraordinary way, just being with this guy seemed to be making a difference. Odd really…

I was still savouring the sensation when he stopped by a shrouded shape.

CALEB

He surprised me by lifting up a corner of canvas to reveal a shiny black vehicle panel.

"Hey, come and check this out." The man was obviously enjoying this, and he drew back the dusty cover with a flourish. Now this was anything but ordinary!

"What is it? That's not junk! No way. That looks new!" I almost stumbled over my words.

It was not new as in the latest model, but its lines showed wealth, class, and richness. It was rare and in mint condition. I couldn't even see what make it was yet, but I could see that it was valuable— very valuable. He pulled the cover back further, revealing the distinctive emblem of a Rolls-Royce in absolutely perfect condition. I was completely speechless. What could I say? What on earth was this car doing in a place like this? I don't know how long I stood rooted to the spot, just staring, transfixed at the car.

Gold pinstripes caressed the sides, and I reached out almost reverently to touch their sweep with my finger. The canvas of the top looked brand new, without a single mark. Deep red, leather seats like lounge chairs invitingly graced the interior. The roomy back had two seats: one facing backwards and the other towards the front. The new smell of luxury was pervasive.

"It's flawless. Like the day it was made!" Suddenly, I became uncorked. Cars! Now that was a subject I could talk about. Especially this one!

We climbed in; slipping into the comfortable seats and the conversation flowed effortlessly between us. Carburettors, brakes, the beautifully crafted timberwork, the exquisite engineering. This was amazing! Each Rolls-Royce was handcrafted to the buyer's requirements making each one a little different, and this was an early 1900's Silver Ghost and she was a beauty!

"We can't get her out just yet. We will need to move some stuff first." The car was parked behind big swinging doors near the front of the building and the thought of going for a drive sent a frisson of excitement through me. I hadn't considered it to be a possibility.

"What sort of stuff?" There didn't seem to be much in front of the car.

He had climbed out of the 'Roller' and was standing holding the door, looking toward the back of the shed.

"Let's take a look. He needs some help back there." He said, nodding towards the ruckus still drifting from the rear of the building.

I felt a strange reluctance to go with him. There was something unknown, and yet familiar about it all. Walking deeper into the gloom, past more of the overcrowded shelves, seemed daunting. I wondered about my response. Why the hesitancy?

Finally, I decided to take the plunge. I had nothing to lose, and besides, I wanted to take a run in the Roller. I climbed out to join my companion and we made our way towards the less than encouraging sounds from the back of the warehouse.

The scene before us was very different to what we had just left.

A young man in grubby overalls was totally engrossed, working on an old Model T. His hair fell into his face, and he impatiently swept it aside. Things were obviously not going well. This Model T was the polar opposite to the Rolls-Royce we had been admiring. Mass produced; there were lots of them. They had the reputation of being cantankerous, crude, and cheap. This particular bucket of bolts seemed determined not to cooperate with any attempt at restoration and the young man responded with equal single-mindedness, violently cursing, and hitting out angrily to bang at the offending vehicle. A spanner ricocheted off the floor to punctuate the latest outburst.

It's amazing what I just knew in this most unusual situation. Here I was standing in the walkway with this man I had just met, looking at a part of myself who was ignoring us both. That's who this was! A part of *me*! The sense of futility was palpable. I could feel his frustration begin to rise within myself. He's trying to get the 'Tin Lizzie' to be like the Rolls-Royce! He's not satisfied with it being a Model T. He's ashamed of it. Like trying to make a silk purse out of a sow's ear, it was an impossible task, doomed before it began. I felt trapped by the pointlessness of the exercise, by the expectations much higher than could ever be met by this sorry looking piece of machinery. It painted a startling picture of my current dilemma. As comprehension dawned, the emotions I was witnessing washed over me in waves. For some reason I could not remain disconnected from this part of myself. I couldn't just stand there distant and unaffected by what I was seeing.

"Caleb." The man beside me called my name. I turned towards my companion and quickly realised that it was the young man he was addressing. There was not a flicker of response from that quarter.

"Caleb." My name was called again, a bit more firmly this time.

"What!!?" He briefly moved his attention from the machinery to the person, not at all happy about the interruption. "Can't you @*&#@ leave me alone? Can't you see I'm trying to work here?"

I could see that he was determined to struggle on, single-minded in his unwillingness to be swayed from his purpose.

"Come and have a break for a bit. You look like you've been at it for a while. Would you like to have some morning tea with us?" The voice was calm and reasonable, unruffled by the emotions blasted in his direction.

I walked over and stood beside the young mechanic, allowing myself to feel the familiar frustration. The Restorer's voice was so peaceful and compelling it drew me to him. Extraordinary.

"Would you like me to help you?" How can I describe the effect of those simple words? It was as if this Restorer bloke was totally, completely believable.

Awareness dawned on my young counterpart's face as his attention was finally caught. I had never seen anything like it. I watched as he was drawn into those deep eyes. I could see the thoughts chase across his face as he considered the man before him. His anger and apprehension gradually, inexorably evaporated like a morning mist yielding to the warmth of the sun. *I can trust him: I can give this to him. I will be okay.* You could literally see it happen! Like a lost child in the maze of a shopping mall when they are restored to their mother's arms. That's what it was like. It didn't take very long before we stepped away from the bits and pieces of car strewn all over the floor, the unfinished project, the impossible dream, towards the Restorer. He embraced us both and it felt as warm and accepting and as natural as a soothing mothers' hug for a little one.

I'm not a huggie sort of person usually, finding any such display a bit uncomfortable, but I found myself responding at a deep, visceral level.

"Well done!" he said. Such simple words but they seemed to melt a primeval knot deep in my stomach that I had not even known was there. Peace infused me. It's hard to find the words to describe it. It was like an oasis of acceptance and tranquillity. It was a place where I wanted to linger. I wanted to imbibe the peace, get drunk on it. It was a place so recently ravaged by the storm. It looked to be having the same effect on the young mechanic. A relaxed grin replaced the perpetual scowl that had been fixed in place when we first met.

When we broke away from the hug, tea and a plate of scones with cream and jam had mysteriously appeared on a nearby bench. Nowadays I usually drink coffee but when I was younger, doing my apprenticeship as a motor mechanic, it was always tea, hot and strong. This was just right, just the way I used to like it. Good sturdy mugs and great slabs of scone smothered in all the decadent stuff. The mechanic's hastily wiped hands cautiously navigated the route between plate and mouth, and successfully stuffed his sizable portion inside without mishap. I had to admit that I wasn't much better. Memories of coming home from school to Mum's fresh baking wafted through my memory along with the tantalizing fragrance of the soft, mouth-watering scones.

The Restorer called for a crew to deal with the car. I have no idea how he did that or where they sprang from. They just appeared! I wondered if they may have been angels, but they were nothing at all like the faded picture hanging on the wall in Sunday school so very long ago. They were completely awe-inspiring. They worked in white gloves, all dressed in pristine white coveralls, and they treated the old rust bucket like royalty. Amazing!

Even a new apprentice would not have such clean clothes when he turns up in his new threads, still with the shop creases in place.

These guys looked nothing at all like newbies…or angels!

The rust was replaced with shiny new panels, black of course, and each part was put in its place, carefully and expertly replaced to form a perfect Model T. It was the people's car, so different to the Rolls Royce, but so suited to its purpose. A car for the masses, Mr Ford revolutionized the infant car industry with his innovative production of the Model T, built so anybody could afford one.

The crew continued their work, sweeping and cleaning until the whole area where the Model T stood was impeccable, as clean as an operating room. The result was astonishing. Their gloves and overalls remained spotless, unmarked by the filth they were eradicating. They had even managed to uncover a window, up high in the wall that allowed light to penetrate the dark back corner.

The young mechanic stood a little apart, watching the proceedings, as if unsure of where he fitted.

"Would you like a new job, Caleb?" the Restorer inquired.

"Yeh, I guess. You've just finished mine! You sure made that look easy." He answered a bit wistfully. He looked a bit lost now that the T was finished. It sat there, having been cranked into life by the crew, as if warming up for a trip to town.

"Let's take a break first up. We're heading out in the Roller parked up the front. Want to join us?" It was an invitation.

I grinned at my counterpart. He grinned back.

"Sure, I think I would like that." He was still a little shy but was warming to this remarkable man.

Space had been cleared by the crew, still spotlessly clean, and the Model T had been moved to sit beside the Roller. We stood together surveying the vehicles. I was struck by the contrast they painted. One was the epitome of simplicity, the other of complexity. If they belonged in the same household they would have very different functions, they were different in what they could do, different in every way. A Roller is a tourer that comes into its own on the open road. The 'T' is the runabout, used on a daily basis, utilitarian and sparse in its appointments— a general workhorse. I was like both, I realized. It wasn't about either/ or. Both were needed. These two cars lined up behind the big swinging door were a statement about my intrinsic and unique value as a person. It was a feeling more than an understanding. It would take some time to distil, to grasp what was dawning on the inside.

I became aware again of my hopelessly tangled sheets and an early ray of sunlight teasing my face. I was smiling. Something had shifted inside me, and I could feel the difference. I could not have found words for what it was that had changed but something had. I went about my day, exhausted but happy, the warmth of that hug still with me.

That night I slept for the first time in months.

CALEB

Chapter Two

It was only two days later that I decided to tell Sarah about my warehouse experience. Our younger daughter, Olivia, was away for the evening; this was my chance. *Now, how on earth do I tell her about the warehouse dream or whatever it was?* I stalled in the doorway leading into the living room of our home, almost changing my mind. I leaned against the doorframe where I could watch my wife as she worked on her knitting, her short dark hair framing her face.

Sarah sat perched on a kitchen chair on a square of old mat in front of the newly installed wood heater, a standard lamp, and the fire bathing her in a soft glow. She had created a haven for herself in front of the heater, a clean, warm patch in the midst of a house covered in dust sheets and chaos, a sanctuary during the renovation. Beyond the aura of light our blanket swathed lounge suite sat unceremoniously shoved into the corner of the room surrounded by boxes and bits and pieces of our lives. It was a mess. There was nothing finished or ordered anywhere in the house.

CALEB

Dinner had been frozen pizza heated in the microwave. Anything more exciting was impossible at the moment. Most of the kitchen equipment was packed away in boxes and there was no proper stove. The sink consisted of a plastic container inside an ancient concrete laundry tub and the dishrack sat precariously perched on the washing machine. Our makeshift kitchen made preparing meals difficult.

She used to experiment with culinary delights from all around the world but not now. It was hardly surprising.

I hope she can get back into cooking when this is all finished. I miss her meals. I thought. *This reno must be making things hard for her. A lot of other women wouldn't put up with all this.*

Sarah seemed unaware of me standing in the shadows observing her and I was left to my ruminations.

She was good for me, I realized. I had given her a pretty hard time early in our marriage. I had no more clue than a toddler playing with a butterfly. She described it as more like a vacuum than a relationship. We had both been miserable. Our relationship had gradually improved since then but recently I had been shutting her out. It wasn't helping things between us.

I couldn't see them in the lamp light, but I knew that her dark hair had a sprinkling of grey and the odd wrinkle now creased her face. A bit cuddlier than when we married almost 30 years ago, she was still beautiful to me.

My mind wandered and I smiled as I thought of our girls. Aurora and Olivia look so much like her. They are like two peas in a pod. They are just as beautiful as their mother, sharing her golden skin tone and dark hair. My Northern European fair hair and complexion didn't get a look in. You couldn't tell that they are two years apart in age. The girls tower over their mother, much to their delight. That's where they took after me—I'm a lot taller than Sarah.

I wonder who they will end up with. Australia is such a melting pot of cultures. Their partners could be from any corner of the globe. I hope they do well. I'm glad Olivia only has a few months of high school left. The chaos and disruption can't be helping her studies but she doesn't complain. She is as patient as her mother. I think Aurora rang her mum today. I must ask her how she's going. Why did she choose college in Sydney? I couldn't wait to get out of there.

People told us we were mad buying land in the Southern Highlands; that we should stay in the city. No one could dissuade me—I loved the Highlands. It's where I felt alive, like I could breathe. It was cooler than Sydney and much less humid; perfect for me.

Building our first house—paying it off quickly—I was proud of my achievements. We did all right financially in our early years. We both worked hard and saved even harder. When the new freeway made the property prices soar, we went again, this time renovating, and made even more capital. I am a plodder rather than a highflyer, but it had paid off.

There have been a few ventures over my time; from selling and installing wood burning heaters—when the girls were little—to making bespoke gates and fences. Pity about the cheap imports that started coming in—that was a good little business. In between, I found work wherever I could—welding, home maintenance. I could turn my hand to almost anything—almost. More recently it had been more like a financial rollercoaster than anything else. The share trading had left me feeling pummelled and drained. Then there was the renovation; this big, overcomplicated, drawn-out, messy renovation.

I had money put aside for the building work and a set amount for share trading but there wasn't an endless supply. Sarah had chosen to step down from full time nursing, working only occasionally so she could be available to help me on the renovation. I knew we were going to miss her income.

My rapidly cooling hands and feet interrupted my musings and I moved to pick up a chair and sit down in front of the fire. Sarah glanced up and smiled in my direction before returning her attention to her knitting.

Beyond the oasis of warmth, the howling, winter wind whistled under the house teasing years of accumulated dirt from between the recently exposed floorboards. We had pulled up the worn, filthy, shag carpet with its uninspiring, brown pattern, hoping to use the original flooring. No such luck. It was irredeemable.

I had demolished the ineffective, old chimney that had dominated the room and the hole into the ceiling was covered with thick plastic that seemed to inhale and exhale in rhythm to the gale blowing outside. Daily instalments of demolition and building evaded Sarah's valiant attempts to control the dust: brick dust, plaster dust, old dust, and new dust.

If I don't say something soon it's not going to happen, I derided myself. Olivia wasn't going to be out forever.

"Sarah?"

"Hmm?" She glanced up from her knitting, her reading glasses perched on her nose.

"I need to tell you about something."

"Sure. Just let me finish the row." She continued counting her row, part of a lacy pattern for a scarf she was making. The soft alpaca yarn was being crafted into a work of art.

Sarah laid her knitting and glasses aside and turned towards me.

Umm . That's a good start, I thought.

She looked at me expectantly.

"Ahh—I had something unusual happen." I petered out, remembering the head spin that the whole experience had been, and I wondered, again, how my wife would respond to my story. I almost lost my nerve, nearly told her it was nothing, but I had gone too far to back out now.

"I met someone—well I think…" This was hard.

The black plastic snapped taut as the hole in the ceiling heaved a loud sigh.

"Start from the beginning. How did it start?" Sarah prompted me, ignoring the disturbance.

Slowly the story unfolded bit by bit. She took it all in, asking about 20 questions, none of which I could answer. She was fascinated by the man I had met, the mechanic, the angels, and the cars. In fact, she grabbed a writing pad and wrote it down for me.

The fire had died down as we talked allowing the draughts to steal the warmth. I stood to refill the slow combustion heater and we watched as it flared, flames curling around the logs.

I wrapped my jacket closer around my shoulders against the cold as I perched again on my chair. We sat in companionable silence as we waited for the fire to take hold, listening to the sounds of the wind.

It dawned on me how little of my early life I had told her before. We had been together since our 20's; our children were almost adults but for some reason it hadn't come up before. Why hadn't I done that? Why hadn't I told her more? I had no idea. I only had snippets of memory—there were big gaps—maybe that was why.

"Thank you for sharing that with me." Sarah's voice broke my reverie.

Her warm response really helped me accept that somehow this was real. Whether a vision, a dream, or a trance of some sort, it was nonetheless real.

It felt good for her to know.

CALEB

Chapter Three

It didn't take long before life returned to its normal routine again. Decisions: dealing with trades people, paying bills, all the mundane, ordinary things. Gradually the memory of the warehouse faded.

In the months that followed, the shares that I had purchased, that had caused so much angst, finally turned a corner. I wasn't out of the woods yet, but it was now slowly going in the right direction: up! It made it easier to forget.

Despite being a full-time farmer, my father had successfully traded the share market. He was a long-term trader, basing his decisions on his careful, daily perusal of the financial press and his trusted broker. I, however, had lost trust in my broker and had decided to go it alone.

My approach was different to my dad's. Unlike Dad, I was reading the computer-generated charts to make short term trades. Everything about it was easier; especially losing money. Most of the time, now, I did okay, nothing earth-shattering, just steady. I carefully watched for the turns that indicated it was time to buy or sell. That is, unless I bought a 'dud'. Over time I had collected a couple of 'dogs' and my latest trade looked set to join the kennel. I had an amazing knack for switching off to the unsuccessful trades. My capacity to avoid looking at those 'puppies' was amazing—until I tried to sleep. I knew what I needed to do. Doing it was another matter. I couldn't understand why it happened so often. Why did I ignore those trades when they turned against me, instead of using the stops and heeding the warning signals? I *knew* what I was supposed to do! It wasn't like it was a huge loss this time. It was just another one. It irked me.

It was during another nocturnal, sheet wrangling, frustrating wrestling match with sleep that I remembered.

Asthma gripped me in its unrelenting vice. Startled, I awoke from sleep into heart-pounding desperation. The helplessness overwhelmed me. Always the panic made it worse.

It had been one of those stifling, still summer days when the heat pounds at your senses making it almost impossible to move. I had finally drifted off when it had happened. I never knew when it would strike.

"Mum, get the Doctor. Please, Mum!" How could I get through to her? I was just a toddler and getting the message across was so difficult. I didn't know the words. Mum's soothing had no impact on the relentless onslaught of breathlessness. "Mummy! Mummy!" The asthma had ambushed my sleep, pouncing on me without warning. It stalked me night and day, never far away. The monster that I tried so hard to deny, to pretend wasn't there, had succeeded yet again.

Please help me. You can fix it, can't you Mum? Please don't leave me here like this, I wordlessly implored her.

I despised my helplessness, the need to rely on someone else, and the terror of being alone, of dying.

The doctor came that night. He had pulled his pants on over his pyjamas and come, the injection he gave me almost instantly bringing relief.

"Is it real or is he putting it on?" he had asked Mum but when he heard that I was standing up at the open window gasping for breath he had come quickly, one of many such visits during my childhood.

The memory of that night so long ago came flooding back with sharp clarity and I tasted the terror again. I have lived my life avoiding pain, running from it, denying it. *That's why I ride losing trades down into oblivion.* The thought seemed to come from nowhere. It jarred but I knew it was significant, that I needed to take notice.

I remembered the man in the warehouse and how he had helped me. *Could he do that again? Last time I had prayed—maybe…*

"God, what's this about? You've gotta help me. Please?" I groaned into my pillow.

CALEB

Chapter Four

Instantly I was back in the warehouse that represented my life. The same man was there welcoming me with a bear hug, his touch and voice calming the night terror. It was so good to see him again.

The young mechanic was also there and smiled shyly at me. He dug his hands into his overalls as if to pre-empt any uncomfortable physical contact.

As we pulled apart, the man who called himself the Restorer drew my attention to a shapeless blob partly hidden in the shadows under one of the broad shelves. A rough cloak of some kind surrounded the lumpy form. There was no indication of anything human about it until suddenly a little head popped out from among the folds of the course fabric. It was a pale little boy in some sort of weird disguise. He looked to be about 5 or so and completely dismayed at being found out.

"Hello, little man. What are you doing here?" I asked him. He looked at me with big blue eyes, as if imploring me not to hurt him. Once again, I knew that I was encountering a part of myself that I had rejected.

"What have you got there?" I could see that he had a collection of stuff he didn't want me to see. It took a bit of coaxing but, finally, he responded.

"This is all the stuff you didn't want. I've kept it for you," His voice was timid, hesitant and defiant all at the same time. "You didn't let me play." The bottom lip dropped as the words slipped out. "You pushed me away."

I realized that I was an expert at pushing things away. *I don't want to think about that just now—so I don't. Simple!* A certain order had been created by pushing things under the rug, out of sight, out of mind but, if I was honest with myself, I also knew that it had created its own mess and difficulties. Just ask Sarah. She has told me often enough. With a start I realized that this little one was lumbered with all the things I was avoiding, the painful things I worked so hard to forget about. They were a heavy burden hunching him over like an old man, the accumulation of years.

I didn't know what to say.

I knew the little one needed help. So did I. I turned to the Restorer, wondering if he would, if he could? His response was immediate, his eyes crinkled with warmth as he spoke. He hunkered down to eye level with the little fellow as he spoke to him, coaxing gently.

"How would you like to give me all that stuff you've got hidden under there? Then would you like to come for a drive? We are going out in the Roller parked over there. Do you know the one I mean?"

The little one didn't seem at all sure about the proposition, scrunching up his nose as he considered it.

"Is he going too?" He pointed an accusing finger at me.

"Uh-huh."

"Sometimes he's not kind."

"Yes, you're right. Sometimes he's not so kind." I winced inwardly at his words. I knew it was true.

"Can I keep my Teddy?" The battered, one-eyed bear hung upside down, clutched close in the boy's arms.

"Sure, you can. That's a good idea."

"I don't like being left behind, but I like going in the car."

"So do I! It's fun, isn't it?"

"What colour is it?"

"It's black with burgundy red seats. Do you know what colour that is?"

The little one nodded, already forming his next question.

"Can we go fast?"

The man winked at him, a cheeky grin spreading to infect all of us with anticipation.

As I observed him interact with the little one, I wondered if I could have given Aurora and Olivia more. I had stayed mainly in the background of their lives, leaving the raising of the girls to Sarah. I remembered how I used to watch my father-in-law play with our daughters when they were little. Unlike my own father, he did it so well. They were always excited to have Sarah's parents visit. Her mother was soft and gentle, much like Sarah, and her dad was fun. He was always up for a horsey ride or some other shenanigans with the girls. After he had gone home, I would get down on the floor to practice playing, feeling awkward and clumsy. I had tried so hard to do it differently to my own father. I'm not sure I succeeded.

The girls were grown now, blossoming into beautiful womanhood. Olivia had finished her final exams and moved away from home as her sister had done earlier. Her college was even further away, in Melbourne. They felt so far away. Maybe it was too late. Those girls had melted my heart but, would they ever know how I felt?

The little one began to push the collection across the space towards us as each of his questions was answered, wriggling as he did so in an attempt to come out from under the weighty fabric.

Restorer's response was to lift the heavy cloak, taking the load so the little one could slip out from under the burden.

CALEB

He jumped straight up into the man's arms without a moment's hesitation. All his reluctance had melted away. He jiggled up and down with excitement and began running his little fingers through the Restorer's hair. I was a bit horrified at the familiarity. I glanced across at the mechanic. He had a huge smile and seemed unperturbed by it all. Kids shouldn't do that to strangers—someone they had never met before! Mind you, this guy seemed to have a very unusual effect on people, like no one I had ever known.

"You're curly!" The kid exclaimed with infectious delight, continuing to jiggle. The man laughed out loud, a deep, pleasant sound that echoed through the cavernous building, transforming the atmosphere, lifting the gloom.

"Let's go for a drive," he said and grinned. I was tempted to join the little one's squeals of delight but managed to contain my own excitement. This was going to be awesome!

"We're going for a drive; we're going for a dri-ive." The sing-song voice showed none of the earlier hesitation.

The four of us headed back towards the Roller, the Restorer making big bouncing steps that did nothing to settle the childish glee. But then I don't think he was even half trying; he was having too much fun himself.

I pushed open the big, wooden, barn doors and then we bundled into the stately machine, fit for royalty. Restorer slipped in behind the steering wheel with the little tyke almost on top of him, still clutching his Teddy. The mechanic and I surrendered the front seat and took our places in the back. My grin continued unabated for several kilometres as we purred our way through the streets. This was the perfect touring car and I lapped it up, savouring the moment. The little one chatted nonstop, more intent on the driver than the drive. He was making the best of the attention. Occasionally, he threw a glance in my direction over the back of the seat, cautious and resentful. There was no room for conversation with that going on. I couldn't get a word in edgeways! Even talking to the mechanic beside me in the back seat was infuriatingly difficult. Frustration began to nibble away my enjoyment, each squeal and interruption adding to the annoyance.

Painful little tyke; I'll have to watch him. What's he here for anyway? The thought swallowed the last of my pleasure.

As if in answer, a flood of understanding came.

I had resented the asthma and the limitations it set for me. If it could have been conquered by pretending it didn't exist, I would have defeated it in a flash. I certainly tried. I hated being told "You can't do this. You shouldn't do that. Come inside now, it's getting dark. Put a hat on, you'll catch a cold. Be careful! You might get sick. Slow down, you might fall. You can't do that, you might get hurt! Something bad could happen." I had lashed out in anger and thoroughly rejected any thought that would say 'I can't'. It wasn't just rejecting the voices of the naysayers and prophets of doom—and my Mum—it was also the little voice on the inside.

He's the little voice. He's 'I can't'. He's the one who always wants to play it safe. The thought was not pleasant.

I looked around at the others. The mechanic seemed lost in his own thoughts, gazing out the window and the little boy, finally quiet, was slumping towards sleep.

He's concerned that I will reject him; that I will kick him out! I've done it often enough before, I guess.

It had felt like this tot, this part of me, had been trying to hold me back all my life. I wanted to get going and the little one wanted to play it safe, so I simply left him and his negativity behind. No wonder the kid looked anxious. 'I can't' was certainly a scary place. He had always been in the background, skirting around the edges of my life.

I don't know how long I spent in reflection but the next thing I knew we were gliding back through the big swing doors and came to a stop beside the Model T.

I glanced across at the man who called himself the Restorer. I could feel a hollowness in my chest.

"Hey, what's happening here? Why am I feeling like this?"

Restorer swivelled in the seat giving me his full attention. It was as if we were the only ones in the car.

"There is a division inside you, Caleb. You have lost sensitivity by rejecting this part of yourself. There are times when you have walked into traps when you haven't listened to your heart."

"I feel like he holds me back." The little noise maker now lay peacefully sleeping, sprawled across the front seat, Teddy clutched in his arms, totally unaware of our discourse. A flash of irritation coursed through me again. "Sometimes it feels like everyone wants to hold me back."

"Has it been working for you?" The question was kind, but it stopped me in my tracks.

I shook my head realizing that so many times my push-through attitude had left me in a mess.

"He sees things that you can't see. He can see the risks and has an eye for the detail, to see the things that need to be worked out in relationships and other areas less obvious to the hands-on, practical part of you that just wants to get on with it. You are not complete without him."

"It still feels like he would hold me back," I grumped.

"Yes, sometimes he will. But on the other hand, he will run with me, now, and together you will go much further than you ever would apart. He will hold you back where there is danger. He is like a safeguard, a watchman. He will help you."

I thought again of the oversize cloak the little one had been hiding in, complete with all the stuff I had been too impatient to look at. Things I had overlooked and discarded; so much stuff I hadn't been willing to know about. I had missed so many warning signs, stumbling blindly into danger.

"You're right. I do need him. I have been doing this all my life. It's a pretty strong pattern, I think." His words were hitting the spot and the light was finally going on.

"Together we can do it," Emmanuel responded.

"Who are you?" It seemed a bit late in the day to be asking but the question I had been avoiding since I first met this man burst out with all the social aplomb of my best teenage clumsiness.

He chuckled again. "I go by several different names."

"So, what did your Mum call you?" I continued digging the hole. Good-natured laughter answered my ill-mannered query.

"You can call me Emmanuel." The name was said with a musical lilt, evoking the fragrance of some distant spice bazaar, or the pleasure of a secret garden shared only with the closest of friends.

"Emmanuel. I like that." The name was mangled by my Aussie accent until not a trace of the exotic remained.

CALEB

Chapter Five

Gently, Emmanuel woke the little fellow and stood him up on the seat so he could see me. His big eyes were aware that something was different. A shy smile crept across his face until it encompassed his whole being.

"Can we play a game now?"

"Let's get in the back so we are all together."

At Emmanuel's suggestion, the little 'watchman' rolled himself and his teddy over onto the rear facing seat. Emmanuel also joined us in the back. Pandemonium ensued; tickling and rumbling in a most irreverent way; absolutely not the way to treat a Rolls Royce! Squeals and giggles erupted in every direction. I still wasn't very good at play, so my attempts were a bit stilted, a careful excursion into uncharted waters. I did more watching than joining in, but this seemed to be for the little ones benefit more than mine. The others seemed so engrossed they didn't even notice my discomfort and even my clumsy attempts were well received. The mechanic was more relaxed than I had ever seen him before, throwing himself into the game.

CALEB

I could see now that the little one had always wanted to join in, but I had pushed him away— always. I had perceived him as 'I can't' but now it seemed that he was much more than that. He was another dimension of me that I hadn't been able to access because I had shoved him aside.

"Emmanuel, who is he really?" I managed above the ruckus.

"His name is 'Commander,'" he answered.

"Really? How does that work?" I was incredulous.

"There is more to Commander than meets the eye." The one in question seemed to be everywhere, bouncing, and laughing, climbing on the seat, on Emmanuel, on the mechanic, on me. Before he had been on the outside but now he was right in the middle of it. His toy bear hit me square in the face. He was starting to get annoying again. I wondered how Emmanuel would handle all the carry on, but he just joined in, laughing, and carrying on almost as much. Emmanuel did refrain from jumping on the leather seats, however. Between bursts of mirth and banter, he continued to answer my question. "This little one will bring fun and joy back into your life."

I was not impressed. "I'll never get anywhere if I muck around like this. You have to focus, surely! You don't achieve anything if you don't do the work. I've learnt that all my life! This looks like play, play, play. This doesn't make sense! Sure, it's fun; but come on!! We need to get on with it!" I ranted.

"Get on with what? You need to lighten up, Caleb." There was no malice in Emmanuel's words, and his eyes were kind.

That pulled me up. My bluster evaporated in an instant. This whole thing was throwing me completely off balance. It seemed frivolous and worthless, just a waste of time, all this play nonsense. I could feel the internal conflict. *God, this is hard.* No sooner had the thought crossed my mind than I remembered the old blue tractor.

I was only a little tyke, maybe 2 years old, and very excited to be up so high,

standing in front of Dad on the big blue tractor. He had his hands over mine, very much in control. Of course, at that age, I wanted to do it myself. Not a chance of that. The whole experience was terminated almost before it had begun. Dad was busy. I was holding him up. There was no room for doing something just for the sake of it, for the fun of it, something that had no purpose. There was work to be done! There was no sense of connection that day, no bonding, and the joy was very short lived. The memory brought with it the sour taste of disappointment and sense of loss and disillusionment I felt so often as a child. No time with Dad was ever play time.

It was not the last time I rode the tractor. I asked whenever he was using it, but it was always on Dad's terms, always very businesslike and distant. I learnt pretty quickly not to muck around on the tractor. If you wanted to ride you stayed very still and very quiet. This was not playtime. No way!

Slowly my focus returned to Emmanuel's face. It was full of reassurance.

"What do I do?" My voice sounded stilted and hoarse.
"Give the boy a hug. It will do you good." Emmanuel's answer held promise and hope.

Woodenly, I turned towards the little Commander. Then the internal Ping-Pong match began. "What are you thinking? You don't have time to play. Cut it out! He'll just get in the way; he's a nuisance; a distraction. He will slow you down."

Why is it so hard to simply give the kid a hug? I wondered.

Suddenly the pain welled up and spilled over and I was able to pour it all out. Words tripped over themselves in an attempt to find expression. It wasn't just the tractor. I felt like a cork bobbing around alone on the ocean, adrift, aimless, just a piece of worthless flotsam with no one to turn to, no one to help. The despair, the longing, the pain, tumbled out into the safety of Emmanuel. He seemed to absorb it into himself, sharing it with me; understanding, caring, and I knew I was not alone. For the first time I knew, I *knew* I was not alone. Emmanuel was with me. I hadn't realized how much I needed to be heard and understood—really heard. When at last the emotional tide had subsided into peace, I was able to turn my attention to the little one. He had waited patiently throughout my outburst, quietly leaning against the mechanic. Tearfully, I scooped up the little fellow into my arms and held him. He wrapped his skinny arms around my neck and clung to me as if his life depended on it. Love, warm and embracing, wrapped itself around us, surrounding us, enveloping, and invading us with acceptance and approval. I was overwhelmed. It was life changing, healing, wonderful love. It was what I had really needed, what I had been missing out on.

"Can we play ball, huh? Can we? Can we?" The strident little voice broke into the moment. Amazingly I was not irritated by it.

I grinned. "Let's do it" The back of the Roller, although spacious, is not exactly built for a soccer match but we attempted a wonderful, four-sided game until we could no longer continue for the side-splitting laughter that overcame us. The laughter unravelled a deep, pent up, tension-filled space inside me.

I emerged tired and peaceful, still brimming with the love that poured into me for days afterwards. It seemed to cascade over Sarah as well as I relayed the events to her. My description of our soccer match really tickled her. She started giggling. Once she starts, she can't stop!

"I could just—imagine you…" She lost it again.

We ended up laughing together for some time.

Chapter Six

The renovation was progressing well. The drafts and gaps were being slowly conquered. Spring had been slow in coming. Brisk, westerly winds and late frosts had extended winter's reach and we were glad of the improvements. We had finished three bedrooms and a bathroom, one wing of the house, and had turned our attention to the next phase. We were moving some internal walls and building up the floor in the attached garage to create a master bedroom with ensuite and robe. By the time I finish with it, no one would be able to guess that it had once been a garage. I was finally starting to feel a sense of accomplishment.

A perfect sunny day, without the incessant wind, enticed us to take the day off to enjoy the pleasant weather and some relaxation.

The Highlands were at their magnificent best. Trees that had been naked during winter were fresh and green with new growth. Blossom trees, azaleas and rhododendrons showed off everywhere you looked. Homeowners had taken great pride in their manicured lawns and impressive gardens and the public parks blazed with riotous colour. I drove the few kilometres into Bowral so we could visit one of our favourite cafés and check out the garden displays in town. This was going to be good.

Visitors flock to our district from miles around, especially on the weekends. We had chosen a weekday thinking it would be less busy, but parking was still hard to find. I cruised around a second time before I found someone leaving right on the main street. Sweet! I lined the car up for a reverse park. I almost always get it perfect on my first go. Not this time. It took me three goes. By the time I had finished I had an impressive queue of cars banked up behind me.

I felt a bubble of irritation, but I held it back. I did not want the day spoiled. Our favourite café? Not today! It was fully booked.

That's okay. There's plenty more in town, I told myself as I reined in my annoyance. We walked hand in hand, acting like tourists, until we found another of Bowral's quaint little coffee shops. My coffee and cake had just arrived when the electrician rang. How do people know to ring at the most inconvenient time? I had been trying for days to get hold of him, so I left Sarah and walked outside to take the call. When I finally sat down, my coffee was cold, and I dropped a chunk of my cake on the floor. It was good cake, too. I was less than impressed. Just to round the experience off nicely, I stubbed my little toe—hard—on the table leg as I got up to leave the café. I took a deep breath, grateful that I had shoes on, and hobbled outside. By that time, I was beginning to get a wee bit testy. What else could possibly go wrong? I was no longer in the mood for garden displays.

"Do you mind if I drop by the plumbing supply place? There's a joiner I have been trying to get hold of." I asked Sarah.

"Sure. You might as well while we are in town."

It was a wasted trip. They didn't have the joiner. I tried two other places, also without success. The whole thing took ages.

By that time, I was completely over it, so we came home early.

The first thing I did on my return home was to turn on my computer to check my shares. I had placed orders for two promising looking shares early that morning.

"You're kidding! Can't I get anything right today?" My frustration that had been brewing all day, boiled over.

I had missed out by just one tick on both those shares! You should have seen the charts! They had shot up like—like—a champagne cork.

I ended up taking it out on Sarah, irritated over anything and everything.

"Put a hook in it and reel it in! The way you are behaving is *not* okay! I have done nothing to deserve you treating me like that! Cut it out!" she challenged me with arms akimbo.

I arced up, defensive and angry, not ready to admit that she was right.

Sarah flounced out of the room. I knew that wasn't necessarily the end of it.

Later that night, after I had calmed down a bit, I apologized and tried to make it right. We talked for a long time, backwards and forwards. None of the incidents that had happened were very big in themselves—there were just lots of them. My capacity had been completely breached.

I had always known that I was a bit of a perfectionist, wanting to do things well, get them right. I guess that is why I am so hard on myself and on others, particularly my family. I have tended to shy away from doing things if I was unsure about my ability. Odd really. On one hand, I am confident and a risk taker, on the other very cautious, wary of getting out too deep.

As I lay there with Sarah sleeping peacefully beside me, I asked the question. It could have been obvious to someone else but not to me.

"Why? Why do I get so frustrated, God? Why does this keep happening to me?"

∽

Instantly I was in the back of the Roller with the mechanic. Emmanuel and the little squirt were in the front. Emmanuel

craned around looking over his shoulder at me, his face alight. It never ceases to amaze me how pleased he is to see me!

"You're doing really well, you know. I'm proud of you." His words warmed me, and I responded with a grin. "Would you like to go to the circus?" he asked.

"Hmm, I don't know. My last experience with the circus left a bit to be desired." My wry response covered the depth of reluctance I felt.

"Yeh, I know. That's why we need to go there." The words were almost drowned out by the ruckus created by the front seat passenger. No one else seemed to have an issue with it, just me. The mechanic was almost as excited as the Commander. Emmanuel looked at me over the little one's head, and I knew this was my choice. My stomach churned at the thought. My one and only excursion to the circus had left me with no desire to ever go back, but somehow, I knew I needed to face it.

After long moments staring sightlessly in his direction, I made my decision.

"Okay, let's do it, but I don't think this is going to be easy." I knew I had to look at this or remain forever stuck!

∽

The memory came back with sharp clarity. The circus is a very big deal when you are only 4 years old. I was spellbound by the sights and sounds, holding fast to Mummy's hand. The lights, the music, the smells, the animals were all mesmerizing, but especially the clowns.

Their big smiles, masked up and hiding true identities, drew me like a magnet. We filed into the big top behind the crowds of people.

When a clown called for children to come and join him in the ring, I begged my mum and dad to be allowed to go down there. I wanted to, so very badly. My pleading rewarded, I carefully negotiated the big steps leaving my parents behind, out of sight in the glaring lights. I took my place with several other, much bigger kids, feeling very chuffed with myself for being so bold.

This was *fun*! We were held in a contraption that lifted us from the ground and spun us in circles. The clown made everyone laugh at his antics. Round and round we went, spinning and laughing, the clown falling and rolling. It was so much fun!

Nothing prepared me for the shock of what followed. The clown pulled my pants down in the last swinging turn of his machine, leaving me embarrassed and red-faced. I was left deserted, alone, everybody laughing except me. My world continued spinning, a leering world of confusion, painted smiles, mocking, jeering, laughing. The other children quickly evaporated into the bleachers, leaving me to manage my pants and begin the torturous long walk back to where I had left my parents. I was alone and in shock, with no one to help me.

That's what happens if you want something. Be careful what you want. You will make a mistake—mistake—mistake. You can't afford to make a mistake. The cost is too high—too high—too high—alone—hopeless—you're hopeless.

I won't ever make that mistake again!

It's better to stay in the shadows than to risk wanting something. It's safer—safer—got to stay safe.

The accusing thoughts embedded themselves, searing a path deep into my brain, cemented in trauma. The talons of shame and hopelessness dug deep.

As I relived the painful memory, I once again became the little boy who had ventured into the ring. But this time, in the place where I had felt so alone, I discovered Emmanuel. He was there, in my memory!

"Caleb, look at me." He gently intercepted my flight. His eyes drew me, quietening the chaos. His eyes locked with mine giving me his strength. There was no mask here, no empty smile, no mocking. The bright lights and confusion and laughter began to fade into the background revealing the emptiness for what it was. Only Emmanuel remained in my focus, steady and trustworthy. His arms were safe and warm, and he let me tremble against his chest as the shock slowly, ever so slowly, subsided. He seemed to absorb the trauma into himself as peace seeped into my distressed heart.

It took a long while before I could listen.

"God is the only one who can get it right all the time, Caleb. Did you know that?"

I shook my head against his chest in response and he repositioned himself so I could see his face. The words felt like a soothing ointment. He paused for a long time before he continued, letting the ointment do its work, until I was ready to listen to more.

"Being wrong sometimes is okay you know. It's how you learn. It doesn't make you a failure. It's okay to make mistakes; it's no problem if you know what to do about them." He paused again, allowing the words to settle.

"When you 'muck it up', we can fix it together. You can come to me anytime. I'm already there. I know what to do. You just have to bring it to me, and we can work on it together. Then you can move on. Doesn't that sound good?" His eyes captured me in their gentleness.

"I guess?"

"It's about hope. It's not hopeless and you're not hopeless. I'm strong enough for both of us. When you feel weak, then I am still strong, and my strength isn't rigid. Rigid doesn't bend; it can't flex, and it breaks so easily if it goes too far. I will help you be flexible instead. Then, you can still hold onto hope and move to accommodate change even when things don't work out like you thought they would. Caleb, I have good things for you and when I say that, it is the truth." Right there in the middle of the ring he was with me. He understood!

How do I put into words the impact of his words? It was as if 'truth' was speaking, personified… That's it! That's the power of it! His truth washed over me, penetrating the pain, finally evicting the lies that had felt so much a part of me.

What a set up! Nobody gets it right all the time, nobody, except God! Having to be right all the time had set me up for hopelessness again and again, for failure and disappointment. Wow! The truth swept through me in waves, washing over me in cascades of gentleness until I felt free on the inside.

The need to be right and the hopelessness were like a tightly held bundle that I had carted around for all those years. It felt like it was no longer an issue. I could see the set up and, with a great heave of relief, it was as if I pushed the bundle across the space into Emmanuel's arms. He wrapped me up in his embrace, removing the shame, replacing it with acceptance. The sense of relief was profound, leaving me feeling almost shaken in its intensity.

CALEB

Chapter Seven

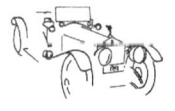Suddenly we switched, and we were back in the Roller, cruising through an old part of town and on into a vibrant, cosmopolitan area, full of life and colour. The other two didn't seem to have missed a beat. They seemed unaware of what had just happened for me. I felt completely drained but it felt good. I felt free. The smile on my face emanated from deep inside. My senses were coming alive, and I began delighting in what I was seeing and experiencing. The couple walking arm in arm, children playing, and the colours and sounds all pleased me. We slowed for traffic, and I watched a young mutt joyfully jump up in a vain attempt to catch the swallows that dive-bombed her, just out of reach. The long-legged dog looked as if she could keep it up forever. The alley where they played was lost from view as we moved on. The conversation in the car flowed between us, easy and relaxed, somehow an extension of the warmth of my smile.

"Come and hop in the front next to me" The invitation came unexpectedly from Emmanuel. The little one made room, and without hesitation, I rolled over the back of the front seat and into the passenger side, a bit undignified and ungainly but effective. We didn't seem to need seatbelts in this amazing car. I liked that. The opportunity to check out the workings a bit more closely was fascinating.

"Can I change gears?" I asked, with the enthusiasm of a little kid.

"Sure," he grinned back, and we worked on getting our rhythm 'in sync' as he worked the clutch, and I manipulated the gear lever. I couldn't remember a time when I had enjoyed such simple pleasures quite so much. There was such a sense of belonging and togetherness. I knew that had a lot to do with it.

We left the city limits, gliding regally down a beautiful avenue of trees in full leaf that seemed to salute us as we passed, and found our way into a quiet park.

A gentle breeze wafted earthy smells around us, ruffling the flowers and causing the leaves to dance merrily. King parrots and crimson rosellas dived between the greenery in flashes of colour. My senses, as if alive after a long coma, took in the heightened sensations and my heart responded. What a blow out! I was overwhelmed at the thought.

Who is this man beside me? He is my friend, and he is amazing!

When we pulled up, Emmanuel produced a picnic basket loaded with food and proceeded to spread a blanket on the soft grass. It was my stomach's turn to respond. I had not realized how hungry I was! Its loud grumble interrupted my sense of awe with a thud, prompting Emmanuel's easy laughter.

"Here, my friend. I have the solution for that little problem," he chuckled, handing me a plate of food. Oh my! What food! Cheeses, olives, cold meats, and goodness knows what else. I had never experienced several of the things on offer. What a feast! Conversation quietened into companionable silence while we devoured the contents of the basket. The little one was soon full and proceeded to chase butterflies around in circles while the three adults rounded off the meal with a perfect glass of red wine.

"Would you like to drive her?" The casual question was tossed in my direction.

"Would I? You bet I would!" I enthused, jumping up to head towards the car. Quickly I doubled back to help Emmanuel repack the picnic basket. There I go, acting like a kid again! I was amazed at my reaction. The staid, careful adult enjoying the anticipation of a treat with the delight and openness usually associated with small children. A bubble of joy burst inside to spread a grin across my face that almost hurt. It was a long time since I had experienced these emotions. Emmanuel was relishing my pleasure as completely as he had shared my earlier pain. His grin matched my own.

I slipped in behind the steering wheel and Emmanuel took the passenger side. The little Commander and the Mechanic sat in the back. I savoured the feel of the timber under my hands. She started immediately, purring into life, sending a shiver of expectancy through me. *This was going to be good!* I closed my eyes and breathed in the smell of opulence. *He's letting me drive it! Wow! I can hardly believe it—that he would let me do that!* I was amazed and overwhelmed yet again.

His voice broke into my thoughts "She's yours, Caleb," he said calmly, with a matter-of-fact attitude. My eyes snapped open to stare at Him.

"What do you mean?" I blurted in confusion.

"The Roller; she is yours," he reiterated.

Was he serious? As if in slow motion the realization began to dawn. He was giving me the Rolls Royce! The best, most beautiful car I could ever imagine. I was stunned! I stared at the elegant 'Spirit of Ecstasy', her flowing gown exquisitely fashioned, the radiator mascot that so beautifully graced the bow of this extraordinary vehicle. The Roller! Mine! Could it be? This was something beyond my wildest dreams; I had never even imagined such a thing. It was mine without striving or pushing and shoving to get it. I hadn't even asked for it and he was giving it to me. *Was he really trusting me with this?* The thought overwhelmed me. Tears began to trickle down my face in a steady stream. Nobody had ever done anything like this for me before, not ever.

Long moments passed before I could turn to face him. There were no words, I simply could not find any, but he seemed to understand perfectly.

That night I held Sarah for a long time. She seemed a bit surprised but after a bit she relaxed against me and just enjoyed the moment.

"I could get used to this!" She mumbled against my shirt front.

"He calls himself Emmanuel." I said after a while.

"Who does?"

"The Restorer guy."

"That's interesting. You know who else calls himself that?" Sarah shifted herself so she could see my face.

"Yes—If it's him—he's not what I thought he would be." I mused.

"How?"

"He's more—I don't know—normal—if I can say that?" I was struggling to find words. "He's—just different—he's incredible." I petered out.

"He seems to be helping you."

"Yes, I think he is." Emotion welled up as I remembered his gift. Yes, he was certainly helping me.

Slowly the story unfolded as I relayed what had happened.

"I noticed the smile on your face, and I wondered what it was about. Thank you for sharing." She smiled up at me, still in my arms.

Chapter Eight

"Sarah, have you seen my long spirit level?" It wasn't unusual that I mislaid tools and things in the chaos of the renovation.

"I think it's leaning in the corner of the hallway." She said from her crouched position, sanding skirting boards.

"Have you got a minute to come look out the back with me? We need to figure out what we need to do with it."

"Sure." Sarah stood up and dusted her hands on her already grubby pant-legs.

Together we surveyed the large, concreted area that we hoped would become a usable entertaining zone. The levels were tricky. I tried to explain how water would flow in a downpour and the options for improving the outdoor area. The concrete worked well to divert surface water, but it was ugly and dangerously uneven.

"Maybe we could leave the concrete and build a deck over the top. What do you think?" I suggested.

"That would be enormous, and can you imagine the junk that would collect under there? You would be giving the snakes a place to hide." She was right.

I certainly didn't want to provide shelter close to the house for snakes.

"I was also trying to work out if I could just pave over the top, but the levels don't work. We would end up with trip points."

"What's the alternative?" Sarah queried.

"I could jack hammer the whole thing up but then I mightn't be able to get the water away." I sounded as unenthusiastic as I felt.

"Now, that sounds like lots of fun." She said dryly.

There seemed to be a problem for every solution, with each new idea having negative impacts elsewhere.

"Why don't we just leave this for now? Does it have to be worked out just now? These things usually work themselves out in the end." Sarah knew me well.

It was a great suggestion, but I couldn't just drop it. I mulled over the problem like a dog gnawing away at a bone, getting nowhere. I wanted to get it right.

I spent hours plotting levels and trying to work it out, getting more and more frustrated.

Finally, I decided to ask for help.

"Where are we going?" The little Commander was keen to go. We had not left the spot near the park where we had stopped for lunch.

"Where should we go?" I asked Emmanuel, who was now sitting in the back seat.

"Wherever you would like."

"Yeh, but where do *you* want to go?"

"You can go wherever you feel comfortable." He certainly looked relaxed enough lounging in the back, eyes half closed.

Being in the driver's seat was different to what I had expected. I had not anticipated the turmoil of thoughts, nor the indecision. *Why was he leaving it to me?* I found myself having trouble going anywhere. *I'll go to the wrong place! Get us lost.*

"I don't know where I'm going! I have no idea where we are, and I don't know where you were headed!" My frustration welled over, mirroring what I had been feeling trying to work out what to do with the outdoor area.

"Just follow the road. It's okay, Caleb." Emmanuel was calm and assured.

I, on the other hand, was anything but!

What gives here? Why do I feel so reluctant? This is strange. I couldn't wait to get going and now I'm hesitant, stuck. It doesn't make sense. It's as if I'm scared to move ahead. I'll be on my own. Emmanuel would be there but what if I get it wrong?

When Emmanuel was driving, or we were stopped, having morning tea and communicating, there was no stress; no pressure to perform.

The need to get it right, to make the right decisions and not 'stuff up' this amazing vintage car was huge. It felt like a yawning chasm about to swallow me whole.

I want to stay here but I'm supposed to be driving. I'm supposed to be enjoying this! Isn't that freedom? Having no constraints? Being able to go wherever I like? Come on man!!! What is wrong with you?

I know Emmanuel is with me but… my thoughts were in turmoil.

"Emmanuel?" It was a plea for help.

The memory that intruded my quagmire of emotion came with stark clarity. We had been together in Dad's bedroom, sitting on the end of his bed one Sunday morning when Dad asked me to spell dog backwards. I was about 5 years old, just beginning to learn my letters. This was rare, a snippet of time relating with Dad, but I couldn't do it! I couldn't reverse the letters; couldn't string them together. He looked at me expectantly, repeating the instruction. I felt the pressure to perform, and it made it impossible for me to do it. When I couldn't do the puzzle, the time was cut, finished. Nothing that had happened previously had any value. All of it was washed away in a moment of exasperation.

Abruptly, he stood up from the bed, exhaling a sigh, his disappointment and disgust tangible. He gave up on me. He got up and walked out. When I couldn't work it out, that was the blunt end to it. It was over. I sat there stunned, watching his retreating back. That was the end of my time with Dad. I felt so unbelievably stupid.

Layers of understanding came as I remembered.

You dummy! I'm out of here. That's what it had felt like. Dad's actions screamed it without him saying a word. Even before he left, I could feel his disgust. I was left to sit in it. *Why can't you do anything right? Stupid! You are hopeless!* Something had shrivelled up on the inside as I had doubled over in pain. It had pierced my heart that Sunday morning. I was totally disappointed, disappointed in myself. The pain of it sucked itself into a dark void, an empty space deep down in me taking my self-esteem and confidence with it. All I was left with was a sense of failure and rejection; alone, betrayed, hopeless and without anybody to help, sitting alone and abandoned.

Dad didn't give me the answer either. It would have helped if Dad had got a piece of paper and a pencil. But no, there was no help. Never was there help. No mentoring, fathering, coming alongside; never. There was just the expectation, like a mountain too big to scale, too hard to look at, tacit and looming—always the expectation. It remained there a constant, unchanging, unchallenged presence overshadowing my existence.

That day, sitting on his bed, I made the decision not to try to relate to Dad, not to even try. It wasn't worth it. I shut down. As an adult, when I carefully reached out, trying to bridge the gap, the distance remained. All my growing up there was coolness between us. Something else had come to me on the bed in the aftermath of Dad leaving, something black and ugly, entwining itself around the wound, hitching a ride on my anger.

A cascade of other memories waded through my emotional morass, leaving the same taste of gall in my throat.

Years later he told me that I was putting on a bit of weight. He made the statement and then walked off. No explanation, no encouragement, no sense of connection or caring. Just a bald statement as we passed on the stairs. What did he do that for? There was no answer that I could ever come up with.

Several times he told me in passing that I should buy shares. He had done it successfully over many years. "You should trade the stock market," he would say. He used to get the paper every day and check out his own shares. I'd have a look at the pages of numbers and codes and be none the wiser. I can't remember a single time when he sat down with me and explained anything or walked me through something. 'This is what that means, this is how you do that, these are the pros and cons.' Just the expectation that you arrive; that you know how. I suppose he had a heart for my good, but it was never put across. He didn't, couldn't, teach. He didn't know how to relate to me, just as I didn't know how to relate to him. All my growing up he was distant. He had died at 80 of the cancer that had reduced him to a shell of the man he had once been. It was too late now to get our time back.

When I was on the blue Ransom tractor trying to operate the levers, it was like that too—cut off, cruelled. The anticipation of something good was abruptly cut off. The pattern repeated itself often, packing down the hardness of my heart towards him into an impenetrable fortress.

Understanding came to adult me as I allowed myself to feel the pain and sit with the memories.

CALEB

It is as if I am in two minds constantly; on the one hand trying to live up to Dad's expectations *Get in there and do it. This will be good. Come on Browne, just do it!* On the other hand, I pull back trying to avoid the letdown. Hold back or bail out. I can't have that happen. So, I often pull the plug.

No wonder my trading is so erratic and inconsistent, that I struggle to make decisions.

This is not a good place. My history needs to be rewritten.

Emmanuel is the only one I know who can help me with that. *I wonder if he would be willing.*

But to go there now would expose raw emotion. I felt unprotected, uncovered at the very thought. *If I let it go—I don't know how to do that.* I had felt more emotion in the last little while than I had been aware of in all my life. There had been more introspection, more insights than ever before but it was straight out hard! All my life I had worked on not going there; to bail out quickly at the first signs…

This was so hard.

He has helped me before—

"Emmanuel, I need your help."

Suddenly the dog memory was rewound, only this time Emmanuel was there in the room, aware of everything going on with my Dad and me on the bed. I identified so strongly with little me that it was as if I was reliving the whole experience.

At my invitation, Emmanuel joined us—adult-me, the traumatized little boy and Dad on the bed.

"Would it be okay for your Dad to go now so you can play with me?" Emmanuel asked quietly.

Somehow framed within the question was the need to let my father off the hook, to release him from my own expectation. It was no small thing to let go of 'you owe me' and acknowledge that the approval my little heart had longed for would never be forthcoming. Dad was simply not able to give it to me, not ever. It was a very big thing to let go, relinquishing the tightly held unrequited longing.

Emmanuel, always sensitive, gave this little one the time he needed. Emotions scudded across his face as he wrestled internally for long moments until, with a sigh, he could give it up, emotions I also shared with this little part of me. We grappled together with the futility of demanding that Dad be changed, that he somehow alters the outcome, makes it different. Together we wrestled, we conquered, we let go.

Dad left but this time the focus was on Emmanuel, not the retreating back.

"Let's go down to the kitchen and we can try again," his words were gentle and encouraging.

Together we wandered down the hall to the kitchen where we found some magnetic letters on the old round-fronted fridge. Magnetic letters weren't around when I was a kid but that didn't seem to matter one bit.

Back then it would have needed pencil and paper or chalk, but time didn't seem to be an obstacle for Emmanuel.

D.O.G…O. No, not that one. Little me concentrated on the plastic letters. G.O.D.

He worked it out!

"There! You got it Caleb, well done! What does that say?"

"G—o—d." He spelled it out painstakingly. "God!" he exclaimed jubilantly.

"Yeh, that's right! You got it. Very good working out!"

Emmanuel pulled out a story book from who knows where, the type with lots of pictures and big letters, easy for little people to enjoy. He sat down on the patterned lino floor with his legs stretched out in front of him with the little one leaning against his thigh, intent on the words and the pictures that seemed to come alive as he read.

"This is Wag, the dog. Hello Wag." Even the blue heeler in the picture was smiling at us with approval.

"See the letters? D—O—G. What happens if you turn them around?"

"I know! It's God!" There was triumph in the little one's answer.

The unfolding understanding continued as I identified with this 5-year-old part of me and responded to Emmanuel.

The reality was that without any aids, Dad's expectations were way too high for a 5-year-old, Dad was much too early. There needed to be a season of training. Missing was the patient development, the coming alongside. It had been a cavernous vacuum in my relationship with my dad.

I could see that Emmanuel was willing to do all that stuff, to show me how to change it around. He was willing to train me, patient while I learned.

I need to forgive Dad. The thought intruded painfully, twisting a knot of anger in my gut.

"If only he had acknowledged he had hurt me! If he had apologized just once! That's all I wanted. Just once! But no; he never did." My words, full of hurt, blurted out of some dark hidden place of their own volition. The little one's face contorted in pain and his arms folded tightly across his chest. We were identifying completely together.

"Would it help if I apologized for him?" Emmanuel's response confronted me.

After a long pause, that seemed to last for hours, I nodded almost imperceptibly, the little one joining me in assent. I didn't think it would help but I was willing to let him try.

"I'm so sorry." His simple words penetrated deeply, releasing the pent-up dam and my tears began to flow. "For what your father did but also for what he didn't do, for what he couldn't be to you." His words began to melt the ice, packed down with eons of hurt and disappointment. He wasn't minimizing or brushing it under the carpet or condescending in any way. He was acknowledging the damage and that what Dad had done was wrong and hurtful.

The blockade was breached and there was no stopping the torrent. Harsh sobs shook both the little one and me as the emotions flowed unrestrained.

My father had shut me out, but I had also shut him out of my life, out of my heart. I had used myself as a whipping post. I had called myself stupid, wearing a track in my brain of self-depreciation. As I released my father, the release was there for me as well. The black thing that had piggybacked my wounding and judgements lost its grip. It couldn't contain me any longer and it skulked away and was gone.

I leaned my head against Emmanuel's shoulder as he held the little one. I felt like a stunned mullet.

It didn't take long before the little one bounced back, eager for life. The little boy that I had left on the bed frozen in trauma all those years ago was now running around outside playing with Emmanuel. He was so happy because he got it right. The little boy got it right! He had help and he got it, and now he was running around happy about it. Squeals of delight drifted towards me from the big back yard as they chased and kicked a ball. I knew I could leave that part of myself with Emmanuel to play and recover. He was safe and happy. My strength began to return as I watched them play.

As I reflected on this, I found myself back at the car, Emmanuel still in the back, the mechanic and the little commander right where we had left them. So much of what was happening to me seemed strange and mysterious; strange and yet normal, for the first time in my life. Normal. There was so much of it that I didn't understand, but to dissect it, to rationalize it, seemed like it would steal the wonder away, or would somehow minimize the sacred into something of the dust.

The place we were parked was right on the city limits and the view offered the first glimpse of mountains in the distance. They drew me like a magnet. I had not been conscious of where this particular route had taken us; but it seemed so right to be heading into the mountains. Affectionately called the 'Snowies' in New South Wales and the Australian High Country in Victoria, they are part of the same mountain range. Certainly, they are not mountains by European standards, but they are majestic, rugged, challenging and so very inviting.

The horizon was lost in a shimmering blue haze from distant eucalypts. There is nothing here of man's doing. It seemed endless, this panorama untouched since the beginning of time. Behind us, the city seemed to be a tangled mess full of trouble and strife; before us, endless possibilities, and open spaces.

Together we soaked it in, the grandeur of the Creator's workmanship.

"It's glorious!" I breathed in the distinct scent of eucalyptus carried on the afternoon breeze.

"Yes, it is, isn't it?" He smiled. "We made it for you to enjoy."

I had to stop to think about that.

He wasn't saying you can have this if—if you do this, if you do that, if you get it right. So much of my life had been conditional, so often I felt like I didn't measure up. This was different. Emmanuel was not saying "You can have all this if…" It was all here, anyway, for anyone to enjoy.

There are opportunities out there. I drank in the thought and, like the view filling my senses, it filled my heart. He is the one who can give me the confidence I have always lacked. It still felt a bit unreal. I still found it easier to identify with the trouble and strife behind us. But something had shifted inside. Dad tried hard. He wanted me to do well but he didn't know how to build my confidence. It wasn't that he took it away; he just didn't know how to give it to me.

"Emmanuel, how do I get confidence now, after all these years?"

"Your confidence comes from me. I'm the one who gives you the strength and makes your world go 'round. It isn't a shotgun approach, Caleb. It is very specific, very deliberate. One step at a time. It takes time. It's not something you hope will stick. Confidence doesn't have the push and shove of trying to *make* something happen the way you want it to. It is seeing what you are going for beforehand, and then sticking with it until you get it, because you know you have it before you start. That's the difference. It is already there. It's a done deal before you even begin. Discipline is your friend to gain confidence. That is the kind of thing you can build on. That's how a person becomes solid, strong, one step at a time."

I recognised that there had been a lot of help, encouragement and patience from Emmanuel, and it had been the step-by-step thing he was talking about. Next time I can build on that. It's not just another situation in isolation, it's a building. *Wow, that makes it achievable!*

My gaze turned towards the distant mountains, softened in blue haze, and I knew where I wanted to go.

"Let's head towards the high country. What do you reckon?" I felt strangely calm and excited at the same time.

"Yes, let's go! Yahoo! We're going to the high up country. High up in the clouds! Yippee!!" The little one certainly seemed to agree.

The mechanic grinned in response.

"That sounds good to me." I could hear the smile in Emmanuel's voice from the back seat.

CALEB

Chapter Nine

A smile of anticipation spread across my face as I selected first gear.

Some of my best memories were of bashing around the bush in an old Fordson bread-delivery van that had definitely seen better days.

The old girl, long since retired, still had the faded 'Buttercup' logo on the sides.

They were good times; hooning around the lonely dirt tracks near my home with one of my mates from school long before we had our licence. The only criterion was being able to scrounge together some money for a bit of fuel.

By the time I was old enough to be put through the hoops by the sour faced man in the motor registry office I considered myself an expert. I am sure that he felt a deep sense of responsibility to protect the community from young drivers with too much bluff, bluster, and testosterone. My friend and I believed he was determined to fail all applicants of the male persuasion whether they knew how to drive or not. He proved true to form and lived up to his well-earned reputation on that first unsuccessful attempt. With my ego somewhat dented I decided to at least read the rule book. My next attempt was successful. I made sure I gave him no excuse to fail me again.

My years working as a mechanic gave me experience with lots of different cars and I was a competent driver, but I still managed to bunny hopped the Roller away from the curb like a complete novice. I depressed the clutch for another try. Better, much better. I would have to get used to this thing. The little tyke delighted at the ungainly take off giggling as if I had performed a stunt just for his benefit. I threw him a sideways glance, not sure whether to be annoyed or not. He seemed able to just enjoy the moment; a carefree little kid with no adult responsibilities; so different to how we found him hunkered down in the dusty forgotten corner. Emmanuel had lifted the awful burden that he had carried for so long, the one that had made him seem like an old man, hunched over with the weight of the world.

I guess I'm pretty intense, very focused, trying so hard to get it right' I'm not much good at having fun and certainly not able to laugh at myself very easily.

It made me realize that mine was not a normal childhood. Besides the limitations of having asthma, there was no play, certainly not as a family. I wasn't able to be a normal boy. There was a very strong example of work ethic, absolutely, but no play, no fun at home. I can't ever remember just having fun with my parents. They both came from farming families who had survived The Great Depression and World War 2. Hard work was a matter of survival back then.

I think that is why the times when I was bush bashing in the old jalopy with my mate had such a sense of freedom but even then, it had been more about a common interest than actually caring about each other. I had been intense then too, and competitive. It was certainly not the carefree fun and delight I saw in the little one beside me.

What is this about? It is not very obvious, at least not to me. What is this?

Even in framing the question, some insight started to come. It seems to happen when I am with Emmanuel.

I realized that I had dealt with most things in life by shutting down my emotions. I had prided myself in the fact that people couldn't usually read me or work out what I was thinking. I had often had a joke at somebody else's expense that only one or two actually 'got' because I was so dry about it. "Browne, you'd be great at playing poker, mate," my friends had commented at different times.

Yep, somewhere I had made a decision to stuff down my emotions, or just distract myself. That's the other thing. My mind dilutes anything that is painful. I'm amazingly good at having my mind race to other things. Sarah struggled with it often. "You're not listening to me," she'd say. We've had a few good barneys over that one!

I remember once she was telling me something about a friend of hers. When I thought she had finished, I got up from the table and got on with the next thing I was doing. When I walked back into the room, I was met by a very emotional woman.

"You just got up and walked out of the room!"

"What?! I heard what you said." I was immediately defensive.

"There is more to listening than just hearing the words you know!" She was livid.

"What did you expect? I said I heard what you said! I had other things to get on with. I was busy." I glanced in the direction of the TV. The news was just about to start.

"Too busy to listen to me?" I knew better than to answer that one!

"I thought you had finished!"

"The sentence maybe, not the conversation!"

"Hmmmph." At this rate I would be lucky to catch the late news.

"I am really upset about what has been happening for Tina."

"There is not a single thing I can do about that." I glanced towards the remote perched on the coffee table.

"I wasn't asking you to *fix* it! I just needed you to hear me. I needed a

CALEB

response from you, your support, not just have you walk out the door on me!" The anger magically dissolved into tears.

There was no use arguing but I still didn't get it. She was an emotional mess over the whole thing. What was I supposed to do about it?

Finally, she tearfully told me that a hug was what she needed. Now that was about as inviting as hugging a polecat! I woodenly opened my arms and she sobbed on my chest pouring out a whole lot more of what was happening for her friend.

Still, it worked, I think. She gradually settled down, but the whole thing took a while.

You guessed it. I missed the news.

It was far from the first time we had had similar conversations.

Now a torrent of thoughts rushed over me.

If I don't feel it, I don't have to do anything about it. I can just keep blazing along; keep going without changing direction. I think everything will be okay because I don't feel the pain—or anything else for that matter— not for myself or for anyone else. It's been my method of getting up and getting on with things.

But then I don't see the signposts along the way either. I shut myself off so I can get on with life without feeling the big blows. I deleted the pain but also deleted everything else when I decided not to let other people in—to block out the pain.

I realized that in all of that I'd also given up some areas of choice.

I think it had been a way of punishing my parents. *You owe me for the discomfort, for all the pain.* It's always been someone else's fault, somebody else that owes me. Sarah has borne the brunt of that one too—and the girls. Many relationships have been destroyed for much less. It's amazing ours has lasted when I think about it.

I've been so harsh, insensitive, and brazen sometimes. 'Keep pushing' has been my answer to cope. It was set up ages ago in the middle of some trauma or other and never taken out of service. I came through the war, survived, but

I am battle scarred. This has blinded me too, hugely; inhibited me and set me up for failure. It's robbed me of discernment and sensitivity. I thought that it was all worth doing so that I didn't feel the pain.

When I think about it, my most familiar emotions are frustration and anger. The range of emotions that I've felt since the beginning of this journey has been more than I can remember having in all my life.

I glanced across at Commander. He was crying. Quiet tears streamed down his cheeks leaving trails through the dust. Lost in my introspection, I hadn't noticed him.

I pulled over to the shoulder of the road and I reached over to where he was sitting and, uncharacteristically for me, pulled him over for a hug. It had worked for Sarah so maybe…

We certainly weren't getting anywhere very fast today.

"Hey little man, what is it?"

"It's the other two; the big boys."

"Sorry, who? Which big boys?"

"Mastermind and Painfree. They're in the back." I spun around to see who these characters were with such unusual names.

"Huh?"

"They keep pushing stuff at me. I don't want that stuff anymore." The clown and the scarecrow in the back looked reproachfully at Commander.

"Emmanuel?" Loaded in my single word was a mountain of questions.

"Hey Dudes." Emmanuel greeted the freaky pair as if it was the most normal, everyday occurrence to have two total strangers suddenly appear in the back seat of the car. Once again, I knew I was encountering parts of myself.

They replied reluctantly, like gawky teens, awkward and self-conscious. Emmanuel took a genuine interest in both.

Painfree was a skinny kid who sported a garish clown suit. His eyes were way too big for his narrow face. A crop of pimples and a thin sprouting of

CALEB

juvenile whiskers added to his discordant appearance.

Emmanuel drew him out, interested in his story. He was the one in charge of using distraction to dodge anything uncomfortable. He had a deal with a big ugly brute that supplied the diversions. It had certainly kept this poor kid very busy. The hideous ghoulish thing provided the distractions and Painfree used them to pull me out of any pickle I found myself in.

To my surprise Emmanuel didn't bag him out for what he had been doing. Instead, he listened to his story and acknowledged that Painfree was quite an achiever, a hard worker who had done his very best to help me under difficult circumstances. That cheered Painfree up a bit, his demeanour lightening at the unaccustomed approval. This thing of running interference had been a never-ending job.

As soon as the conversation began, a hideous demon became visible, exposed by the conversation with Emmanuel. Instead of being threatening, it was whimpering, cowering in the corner.

Very gently Emmanuel made Painfree an offer. It was a new job, working with Emmanuel, helping Caleb concentrate on Emmanuel instead of all the other empty things. He explained that it would construct something—something of lasting substance. I could tell that the idea had a lot of appeal for Painfree.

Painfree sat for long moments mulling it over, before pulling the contract he had made with the demon out of his pocket and handing it across to Emmanuel. With a grin and a flourish, Emmanuel ripped that sneaky, crooked agreement into tiny pieces. At that, the gruesome dark demon fled like a scalded cat. He couldn't stand to be there any longer, gone, banished. No argument, no resistance, just gone!

Emmanuel and Painfree embraced; the muscular, tanned man and the scrawny, pale runt in the clown suit. There was a sense of Painfree finding his purpose. What he had before was a job not a purpose. It was a counterfeit. Now he would be fulfilling his destiny, working with Emmanuel, not just for him. He would be encouraging other parts of Caleb to come to Emmanuel. He would no longer be avoiding the lumps and bumps but walking through them. Not forever blocking by distraction but leading through the maze to the Restorer. Leading through, not diverting from. There was a subtle difference. This was a significant job, and I could see the dignity of it straightened his shoulders, lightening his whole bearing. The new jeans and T shirt that Emmanuel gave him didn't hurt either. He ducked behind some bushes on the side of the road to change and emerged with a grin almost too big for his face as he looked down at his new outfit.

"This was going to be fun! And I get to hang out with Emmanuel! What a *dude*!"

Meanwhile Mastermind had been watching the proceedings with great interest. His faded scarecrow getup contrasted sharply with how cocky he seemed, but he couldn't help being impressed with what Emmanuel had done. He had been there, hiding in the background, when Caleb had met the Mechanic and the little one. He had observed as Emmanuel negotiated with other parts of Caleb and he was very wary of being caught out.

Emmanuel asked him about his job, and he was more than willing to boast about it. It had been a particularly difficult one. He had big responsibilities, weighing heavily on his young shoulders. He had taken it very seriously. His task was to stay in the middle of the road, fending off anything uncomfortable. He was very proud of his achievements. By his own estimation, he had never failed, until Emmanuel had shown up and a few things had somehow slipped through. He controlled what came in and what went out, blocking the extremes and violent swings. All that wild, kooky, unpredictable stuff didn't stand a chance, not with him in charge. He was definitely the boss, the one who called the shots.

"So, what do you do?" Mastermind asked Emmanuel, having given a detailed description of his own role.

"I look after all of creation."

"You do? Coo-ol!!" In an instant he had gone from a smug youth to a wide-eyed boy, obviously very impressed.

He knew the Mechanic, Painfree and the Commander well. He liked the idea of having Emmanuel's help, but no way did he want anything to fall apart.

"Yes, I can see your concerns. We would have to do this sensibly." Emmanuel rubbed his beard in reflection. "You know! If you were lowering someone down with a rope, you wouldn't just drop them, would you? You would let them down slowly, carefully so they don't get smashed. Yeh?" He waited for the tentative nod.

"I won't drop the bundle."

Mastermind was still apprehensive about the whole deal.

"Look at what I have done for the others. You won't find better," Emmanuel continued. There was no swagger in the quiet assertion.

Mastermind eyed Emmanuel cautiously.

"There are bigger and better things that you could be doing, you know."

"What sort of stuff?"

"There is stuff you have been blocking out that we can work with together. That way you get to use the whole road not just the middle. Things that have appeared to be dangerous extremes can be taken on board and utilized. Rather than have them squashed, we can facilitate them and allow them to function. It's kind of the opposite job but in the same industry. You are familiar with all of it but have kept it out rather than including it. It hasn't been proportioned properly. We'll get to work together. It'll be great."

The hesitation was beginning to melt. Mastermind nodded, concentrating on each word.

"You won't have to carry the whole weight on your own. You can refer to me any time. Mastermind, you have been working very well with one thing, so I am going to increase your responsibility—together, you and me. I will not just double the capacity; I will increase it exponentially."

"Wow! Way to go! Let's do it!" The last whisper of hesitancy evaporated in Mastermind's enthusiastic response.

It changed the dynamics in the car having a couple of lively teenagers along, necessitating a seat swap of course. Emmanuel remained in the back now, with the Commander and the Mechanic sitting next to him, while the two boys took over the big front seat. They looked like normal, skinny prepubescent boys now, both dressed in jeans and t-shirts. There was a lot of fun banter and jostling, noisy but full of life. It was so much better than the sullen, introverted boy I had been at that age. I sighed in pure pleasure at the sense of freedom that had come.

Did I understand everything that had been happening? No. I can't say that I did. What else would this journey unearth? How many other parts of me were hidden somewhere? I had no idea, but still it was good! That much I knew. I appreciated all the things Emmanuel had done and what he was doing. It's amazing to me that he cares so much.

Again, I slipped her into gear, realizing we had come only a few kilometres down the road before we had stopped. Did it matter? Nuh. All this was much more important.

CALEB

Chapter Ten

We hadn't gotten very far before I started getting stirred up again. My driving was smoother, but my emotions were not. I became aware of the discomfort of having Emmanuel in the back seat. We had left the town behind and had passed several intersections. Each time I had chosen a well-travelled road that appeared to be heading in the right direction.

It felt odd with him in the back. It didn't seem right somehow. "Just follow the road," he had said.

Why am I getting stuck on this? Emmanuel seems happy whether he is in the front or the back. He just wants to come with us. He is okay. But I'd be so much more relaxed if he was in the front, even more so if he was driving. I don't know what to do; don't know where I am going. It doesn't feel good. I'd prefer to know where I'm going. I don't even know where we are! The city! What city was it? There isn't one this close to the Australian Alps. Victoria— The Snowy Mountains? Where are we? We haven't passed any signs with names I am familiar with. In fact, we haven't passed any signs at all! Where are we?

CALEB

I have visited the high country more than once, driving the wonderful four-wheel drive tracks in tandem with friends. But always, *always*, you go prepared. Maps, recovery gear, chain saw, fan belts, extra food, water; on and on it goes. We met a couple of blokes once when we camped out at Wonnangatta Station in the very heart of the Victorian high country. They had not brought along the proper maps and supplies. It is a spectacular place but it's not a trek for the faint hearted and certainly not for the ill prepared. Unbelievable! Sarah fed them—proper food, not the chips and the couple of cans of fizzy drink that was all they had with them—and we ferried them out in convoy. What were they thinking? They had left Dargo without kitting up! And on their own! Anything could have happened to them, out there, miles from anywhere!

What am I thinking?!

A familiar angst rose as I remembered…

Panic, heart stopping panic gripped me as I went under the water yet again.

I gulped more turbid river water until I surfaced just long enough to let out a strangled yelp for help.

We had spent the morning at the beautiful Coal and Candle Creek in Sydney. I had been in the water most of the time, my nose plastered with white zinc against the burning summer sun. I carefully stuck to the broad sand bar that allowed me to safely stay within wading depth.

Australian rivers are notorious for sudden drop-offs and hidden eddies and snags. A broad section of the creek had been fenced off for safety, but the capricious moody current had undercut the sandbar creating deep holes. I had been very cautious at first, heeding Mum's instruction, aware that I couldn't swim like the big boys.

There was a swing made out of an old tyre hanging over the deeper water. It was tied to a sturdy branch of a patient old gum tree that had seen generations of exuberant kids dive bomb each other from its height. The older children had been occupied well away from the younger ones for most of the time but later they invaded the sandbar where the younger children played. They came chasing and laughing, oblivious to their impact on the little kids. I had retreated from them and their reckless fun, unaware that I was gradually moving closer and closer. Unknowingly, I had stepped backward, and then…

My arms flailed, desperately searching for safety on the treacherous precipice. Everything was in slow motion, each tortured gasp for breath, every wild movement of my body. I could feel the tug of the current increasing, pulling me, drawing me away. No one could hear my cries for help, swallowed up in the laughter and banter of the much older kids, who were completely ignorant of my plight.

Not so my mother. She had been watching and had heard my pathetic cry for help over all the racket. Like a general leading his troops into battle she waded into the fray, pushing the careless youths out of her way. She couldn't swim any more than I could but that did not stop the onslaught. Young bodies flew as she pushed her way towards me, unrelenting in her resolve. Her thin summer shift clung to her, dignity and modesty abandoned to her courage.

She plucked me up, spluttering and gasping. Sweet air rushed into my tortured lungs.

Somehow, she reached the fence and clung desperately to me and the enclosure until help arrived. Her courage had suddenly evaporated, but not her determination.

The whole time my Father sat on the shore.

He could swim.

~

I snapped out of it with a jolt, anger replacing the shock of the memory.

CALEB

"Where are we going?! We can't do this! No maps! No gear! I don't know what you're thinking but this is not good enough!" I went on and on, angry and accusing.

"And why didn't you help me? I could have drowned!" My blustering rant was directed at Emmanuel or my dad or both. I petered to a stop as finally the real question came forward.

"Would you like to have another look, Caleb?" Emmanuel didn't seem at all put out by my explosion.

Gently he showed me: his insistent tug on Mum to get her attention, the angels bringing me to the surface again and again. He had been there the whole time.

When I was under the water, I didn't know what to do. I couldn't swim! If only I had known how to swim! I could have helped myself.

But I called out and help came.

"See? That's how it is now, too. I'm here and you are okay." He paused to let his words settle me.

"I don't want to live your life for you, but I will help you live yours. I have equipped you with everything you need."

I stared sightlessly over the bonnet, considering what he had said. Long moments passed before I could respond.

"I guess you didn't give me the Roller so you could drive it."

"Exactly."

Somehow, yet again, we were pulled over to the side of the road, this time in a broad turn-around.

We clambered out and Emmanuel produced hot tea and warm jackets for everyone. There were also gloves, scarves and old-fashioned peaked caps that looked the part 'to a T' for driving in our vintage car.

He handed me a little bottle, shaped like an animal horn, filled with sapphire blue liquid. It hung from a silver chain and was rather beautiful. I'm not much for jewellery so I absentmindedly put it in my pocket and promptly forgot about it. I didn't even think to ask him what it was. Later, I wondered if I had missed something important in not taking more notice of his gift.

The breeze had picked up, crisp and with the smell of distant snow. It seemed likely to cool down quite a bit as we headed into the foothills.

We sat together on the running board, enjoying the company and the home-made muffins. They tasted suspiciously like the ones Sarah had produced from our supplies to feed those blokes on the track out of Wonnangatta. I bit into the moist cake. Yum, one of my favourites. I glanced across at Emmanuel, wondering if he was having a go at me. He grinned, saluting with a half-eaten muffin.

"Yep; they're one of my favourites too." There was no rancour in His comment, just the sort of banter that happens between the best of mates.

The whole thing was comforting and reassuring: the private joke, the tea, the way Emmanuel had laid the down-filled jacket across my shoulders. All of it told me that I was cared for.

I guess this is about learning to trust. If I knew exactly where we were going, had it all in the bag, I wouldn't need to trust. He gave instruction before when I needed it, so I guess he will continue to do that. He keeps pulling out the supplies too. I have no idea which road we are on, no idea about most things really, but maybe it's okay. One thing I do know: I don't want to go anywhere without him.

The conversation flowed backwards and forwards while the teens chased the boy, running off steam. He squealed and laughed in a way I was never allowed to when I was young. That sort of noisy fun was frowned on. The mechanic joined in, rescuing the little one when it became a bit too boisterous. They were dusty and sweaty when we piled back into the big leather seats to continue our journey.

I eased out onto the road, handling the big motor with much more aplomb as we headed towards the hill country.

CALEB

We passed golden paddocks dotted with dirty, grey sheep heavy with wool. The stands of red gums and box cast long shadows in the afternoon light. The colours of the mountains were shifting in the distance, deeper blues, indigo and violet, preparing for the majesty of sunset. Kangaroos were beginning to stir, coming out of their hiding places, camouflaged amongst the rocks and in the shade of the lonely gums that had survived when the farms were cleared. Later they might wander onto the road, but not yet. *Odd. I haven't seen any roadkill in this trip. You usually see some…*

I found myself beginning to relax, enjoying the scenery and the purring of the big engine. She responded to my touch, seeming to enjoy the drive as much as I was, taking the corners with ease.

This was a most unusual road trip.

Chapter Eleven

"What do you think? Isn't it lovely? I am so happy with this colour!" Sarah enthused, paintbrush in hand. Her eyes sparkled behind paint-spotted glasses that matched the splodge on her chin.

"It looks great." My eyes scanned the room and I smiled at her. It really did look good.

"I'm going to use half strength in the hallway, or I think it will be a bit dark but I love it in here with the north-facing windows." Sarah had spent hours poring over colour swatches and trialling sample pots to get just the shade she wanted. I joked with her that the paint shop would have empty shelves, but she had just grinned at me and kept right at it. This house was going to look amazing.

Sarah has an eye for colour, and she sees nuances that I am completely oblivious to. I don't think it was something my parents could see. When my dad chose the colours the whole house was beige and, after he died, Mum had it repainted. Every room was a different and bright gelato colour. I had no idea that choosing the right neutral was such a thing but if she is happy, I am happy. Her workmanship is generally pretty good too, which is what I tend to notice.

I remembered when we were building our first home, she had tried her hand at painting skirtings and architraves for the first time. I had crawled around the room on all fours until I had found a little run in the paint. There was only one in the whole job but that was what I had commented on. *Why on earth did I feel the need to demolish her? I don't know why she didn't give up.*

She was still here, sanding, preparing, painting, up and down ladders and scaffolding. Her well-worn work clothes gave testimony to many hours of work. She hadn't given up on me.

Patterns that I had dragged into our marriage, downloaded from my parents, were beginning to shift. Dad had allowed very little expression for Mum. He had quietly wet-blanketed her as her father had done before him. At the end of primary school, she took on the care of her invalid mother and the household. Her days were filled with cooking, cleaning, washing and the never-ending needs of her siblings and mother. This arrangement did not finish until the day she got married at twenty-one. It was borne of necessity, not abuse, but that did not make it easier, nor did it help her build confidence in who she was or in her own abilities.

This thing with Emmanuel was starting to make a difference for us. It might seem like a little thing, but Sarah and I were laughing a lot more together. I was even able to admire her work without using a magnifying glass—not that life was always comfortable or easy.

I guess it's a bit like starting a plumbing repair; you uncover lots of crap before things begin working properly again.

When I had finally spilled about the dud trade, Sarah had handled that remarkably well. She had known more than I had realized. She could read me pretty well after all these years.

The renovation was progressing fairly well. We had completed the main bedroom and ensuite and a temporary kitchen, and soon we would be able to move from the cramped, dingy rooms we had been using. Navigating around boxes to climb into bed is not my idea of fun. Cooking had become so much easier with clean, new surfaces and a door to shut us off from the dust. Soon I would build a dream kitchen for her.

I was starting to feel a sense of anticipation and wellbeing. Gee, it was good! Then a series of things happened that left us both unsettled and testy.

The first was a mirror I had hung up in the bathroom. On my first attempt, I had hung it too low, leaving an unnecessary hole in the wall. Sarah had seen me do it and hadn't said a word. She just let me proceed!

"Why didn't you tell me it was wrong?" I had fumed at her.

"You didn't ask me to check. I didn't know it was wrong." She had shrugged. "Just put it up higher. There will always be a mirror over the vanity. What difference does it make if there is an extra little hole hidden under there?"

Another day I was laying pavers for a friend. Sarah had come to join me for lunch and stood for a while watching as I worked, esky still in her hand.

"Honey, I think the angle is heading a bit wrong."

"What do you mean?"

"I don't know. It just looks wrong."

I replaced the trowel with its load of wet mud in the barrow and uncurled myself to stand. I stood back to eye the pavers I had just laid. The curving gradient of the soldier row had gone off course. Darn! Fortunately, the cement had not set hard. I had to pull them out and start again.

I had placed a dozen pavers before she piped up to tell me they were wrong! Couldn't she have told me earlier instead of just standing there watching me?

Women! Fair dinkum!

To top it all off, I felt like I had to watch what the tradesmen were doing at every turn. There had been a few mistakes, a few little shortcuts. *They are here to help me, surely! That's what they are supposed to be doing! Why do I have to be looking over their shoulder? I can't always be there! They are there to make my life easier, not harder! Isn't there anyone I can rely on?*

There was also my share trading. When I had returned to navigating their murky waters, I had begun by taking small, cautious steps. On the whole, I did okay. Confidence was returning. Then I began taking bigger risks, larger contracts, and copping some bigger hits. Now it looked like the latest one was going to turn bad as well. *Not again!*

"Emmanuel, are you toying with me?!" Man, that's how it feels!

"God! I don't know how to do this! Help me—please!"

Instantly I was back in the Roller.

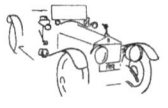 The young blokes in the front beside me looked more than a little rattled, wide eyed and pale. The vehicle still rocked slightly as if it, too, was in shock.

I had been driving the Roller like a sports car and thrown her around the corner too fast, losing traction on the gravelly surface, and skidding out of control. We sat where we had come to a stop only a hairsbreadth away from an ancient railing, facing in the wrong direction. How this had not ended in disaster I do not know. Somehow, no one was hurt.

As the dust plume settled around us, I got more stirred up, eddies of frustration rising out of control.

"I'm sick of this!" I erupted, twisting in my seat to glare at Emmanuel. There was no stemming the tide. "Why didn't you stop me? I could have stacked this thing! Why didn't you tell me that trade wasn't going to work? Why didn't you help me? You're just having a laugh at my expense! You're just toying with me!" There, the angry accusation was out.

I expected him to shrug his shoulders and say "Well, if that's how you feel." fobbing me off, but he didn't. The gentleness in his eyes caused my bluster to begin running out of steam.

"You're doing well, you know; much better than you think. You just forgot to ask me for help."

"It doesn't feel like you care!" I continued. This time, it was a lot less volatile. "I feel like a fool. When am I ever going to get this? I don't know how…"

A memory came flooding back as we spoke.

 The asthma was unrelenting. Nothing brought relief for long. It was repeatedly bringing me undone. The doctor had visited many times and sometimes we went to him but, eventually, he sent me to a specialist in Sydney.

Our farm was near the ocean and the specialist suggested that I be sent away from the salt air, which he felt was my biggest problem. No mention was made of the 'chooks'.

Mum and Dad began to make enquiries. Who could take a sickly, eight-year-old boy?

The arrangements happened around me, somewhere above my head. My future was being determined for me. I heard a snippet here, a bit more there, and gradually I formed the realization that it was actually going to happen. I was going to be sent away.

The thought of being sent away from the farm, anywhere away from the farm, felt like an adventure, exciting in the possibility of being free from the asthma. My parents may not have recognized the impact of the constant dust from the chickens, the privet bush that grew near the back door, or the cat dander, but I knew. Moving as a family was never in question.

The decision was made. I was to spend 6 months in a Sydney City Mission home for boys in Bowral in the Southern Highlands of New South Wales. Arrangements were made to deliver me to Central Railway Station. There I was to be met by a representative of the Mission who would accompany me to my new home.

I don't remember much about the preparation. Mum was a bit flustered as she packed my little suitcase, muttering to herself and periodically reminding me of how I was to behave. Not that I took much notice. Wash behind my ears? Not if there was no one to hound me about it. Not likely.

When the day finally arrived, it was grey and overcast, threatening rain that never eventuated. It was the sort of day that sapped the colour from the landscape. But the sense of adventure had taken hold and it could not be quenched by the bleak outlook. I was going on a train ride! I was going away from the farm! I was going away from asthma!

A middle-aged woman I had never met before greeted us. A grey felt hat was pulled down close over a severe grey bun. The sensible brown shoes clicked loudly as she walked briskly along the platform, holding my hand in the firm grip of one hand, my little suitcase in the other. The prim blouse and dour skirt suit almost obscured thick woollen stockings, all leftovers from a bygone era. There was no colour here, either. She matched the bleak and threatening day.

My mother pulled me close in an embrace. A quick hug for my little sister and a handshake for my dad and we boarded the big old steam train that would take me beyond the range of the electrified city rail lines.

Thick smoke billowed as the train slowly pulled away from the platform, and I glanced towards the quiet figures waving in my direction. I returned the gesture briefly, before swivelling my head, gluing my nose to the windowpane to see the unfamiliar sights. It was some time before I gave my family another thought.

My childish questions were answered briefly by my companion, but her responses did not invite conversation, so I contented myself by gazing at the passing scenery. The city suburbs soon gave way to farms and long stretches of untouched bushland.

Finally, after several hours, the train arrived at its destination. Somewhere along the track the sun had escaped the confines of the cloud cover to showcase Bowral at its best. It was a beautiful sight, and I craned my neck to try to take it in as we walked, my hand once again firmly captured by my carer. Our route led us under the dense canopy of plane trees that had donned their autumn garb. Sunlight and shadows danced merrily across our path, paved with the gold of fallen leaves. The unexpected crispness in the air allowed me to inhale the fresh earthy smells. Here, in this place, I could breathe. Even the long climb up the hill, revealing even more beautiful trees and pretty cottage gardens, did not cause me any distress.

A sweeping gravel driveway led to an imposing two-story brick building. This would be my new home.

My introduction to the facility was a bit of a blur, meeting the manager and other staff, over twenty other boys, mostly older than me, and listening to countless rules and requirements. Exploring the extensive grounds would have to wait. By the time I sat on a hard wooden bench to eat the evening meal I was exhausted. That night I climbed into an unfamiliar bed surrounded by strangers. Any late-night shenanigans were strictly controlled by one of the women whose quarters adjoined the large dormitory style room.

On Monday morning I joined the queue to climb onto the bus for my first day of school.

The other children filed off the bus and quickly disappeared from view. I was left to ask the bus driver which of the buildings I was to go to.

Nobody seemed to be looking out for me. It was a strange feeling, like I was lost, a misplaced bit of flotsam of little concern to anyone. When I finally found an adult to ask for help, I was escorted to a classroom to face even more unfamiliar faces.

I don't remember having a friend, either, in school or in the boys' home during my stay in Bowral. It was every man for himself. As one of the younger boys, I quickly learned to keep my nose clean, 'toe the line', and stay out of the manager's way as much as possible.

He had a commanding voice and demeanour. Any perceived misdemeanour was penalized with punitive harshness. Even the big boys were terrified of him. Three of them had tried to run away but they were returned and made to stand naked in the dining room during the evening meal. I sat quietly trembling, all appetite evaporating, with my eyes averted as they endured the mocking and humiliation.

The cavernous dark brick buildings and polished timber floors echoed my growing loneliness. Homesickness threatened to swamp me, especially at night after the lights had been turned off. The tears were pushed down. It would not pay to cry in this place.

Despite it all, I felt like a real boy for the first time in my life, able to run and play without the shackles of asthma restricting me and stalking my every move. The large grounds of the home and the school yard offered plenty of scope to explore. Weekend walks through the bush to the top of Mt Gibraltar, the 'Gib' or to a local dam to catch crayfish with the other boys were excursions into a new freedom.

The delightful interplay of sunlight and shadows, light and darkness cast by the towering plane trees had disappeared as my stay continued. The trees had shed the last of their golden leaves in a late autumn storm. There was no more gold, just windswept drifts of brown discarded as the weather turned colder. The driving power of lonesomeness threatened to sweep aside the delight of being free to breathe.

My only connection with home was letters I regularly received from my mother. I was expected to reply to each one based on instructions I was given by the dour faced female I had encountered on my first day. Each letter was appraised before it was dispatched. I could not say what I so badly wanted to.

It was about a month into my stay that I hatched a plan. I had to circumvent the system. She could not know. So, I asked my teacher for paper and an envelope. Carefully I wrote my parents a letter.

Dear Mum and Dad,
Plees cum and pick me up. I am very sad and I wont to go home.
Caleb Browne

Fantastic! Now it was just a small matter of a stamp and asking someone to post it for me. I mustered up the courage to ask one of the carers. She was a ray of hope in this place. A younger woman in her thirties, she shared the care of the boys with several others. She was kind, with a gentle smile and a pleasant voice. Surely, she would help me. She smiled and took the letter, promising to post it for me.

That afternoon, as I played with a group of the younger boys, my name was called by the stern-faced manager. I trembled as I responded. I shook uncontrollably as my little letter was read out loud. I was not stripped naked, but I might as well have been. The betrayal and shame were complete. I felt completely helpless and stuck.

A flashback of my cot came flooding in—a memory I didn't know I had. I was so tiny. I could feel the torment, my skin burning with eczema. There had been no relief, none, not once during any waking moment. It started just a few weeks after I was born and continued unabated until just before I had turned one year old.

The doctor's advice, as was common at the time, was followed to the letter. 'Minimal handling' meant my mother could not hold me, could not take me in her arms except to feed and change me. Little mittens stopped me scratching. All the creams, lotions and potions did nothing to help.

During the day, Mum tried desperately to soothe me in any way she knew how. Dad would join her in the evenings, after his work on the farm, to help her with the never-ending, exhausting chore. They would sit on the wide, old

CALEB

veranda pushing my pram between them for hours, back and forth, back and forth. Eventually I would sleep and give them some respite from my crying. Often, even that did nothing, and Dad would bundle me up and take me for a drive in his old Austin truck, bouncing along, its noisy engine soothing me. Somehow, somewhere, I longed for that drive and the blessed relief of unconsciousness.

There was not a thing I could do about it. Nothing I could do to help myself. I was utterly, totally helpless. I was also frustrated, distressed and mad—really mad. Mad at being tied up, unable to scratch; mad at being ignored; mad at not being picked up and comforted; mad at my parents. Just mad!

"Don't just leave me here in this torment!" My adult-self gave the little one the words he had been unable to express.

In the middle of my thrashing and screaming I became aware of Emmanuel, inside the cot. He was standing, like an ancient warrior, between me and a black slobbering demon that was flinching now at being exposed. The spear he plunged through the gaping mouth was made of light, dazzling in its brilliance. I could see the terror of the tormenter as it took its punishment. Emmanuel nailed the thing to the bed with only one thrust. It made fizzling, hissing sounds as it evaporated, leaving not a mark to show where it had been.

Gently Emmanuel scooped me up, a tiny baby in his arms.

Gradually the calm that touched my body also reached the deep recesses of my heart. Emmanuel made low, cooing noises in a language that I didn't recognize, singing a lullaby occasionally, comforting and so very soothing. His face was completely intent as he gazed deeply into my baby eyes. He seemed to have all the time in the world.

Although I was the child, my adult-self also watched, identifying deeply with the little one.

As I did, I also became aware of a blue baby, limp and pale without the healthy bellow of a newborn. I had been born with the cord wrapped around my neck. Again, I was scooped up, still naked and covered in mess. Emmanuel untangled me and then, ever so lightly, did mouth-to-mouth, breathing life.

"Live, little one," he said, and I did.

I became conscious of the Roller again, Emmanuel eyes still soothing me.

"I'm there, you know; always." There was no rebuke in his gentle voice.

I needed a bit of time to recover, and then we talked for a long time, with the Roller still tilted at an odd angle. The little commander had nodded off, his head resting on Emmanuel's lap and the others waiting quietly outside on a grassy slope, aware that I needed the space to be with Emmanuel.

During our conversation it became clear that I had been living my life out of this place of angst, pushing, and shoving to try to make things happen the way I wanted them to be. There had been desperation in my trading, too. No wonder it hadn't been working! It had been a survival thing, to try to get some relief. I'd been bucking the system, not wanting to be tied down. *Nobody is going to tell me what to do!* It had felt like everything, and everyone, was against me—like there was nobody I could rely on or trust. I couldn't remember a time without that.

But knowing better than anyone else hadn't worked. It had set me up. I'd tended to go against the grain just for the sake of it. It had taken me out of the flow and left me on the sidelines again and again. I missed good opportunities, skipping out of trades too early, staying too long in bad ones.

I'd been grabbing and demanding my way through life as if gasping for breath to try to survive. My life had been much more about survival than getting my own way.

CALEB

Together we revisited the memories, Emmanuel and I. Together we looked at the emotions, the things I had come to believe. Together. I was not alone.

The feeling of being totally helpless and alone, and the intense frustration that so often accompanied it, were so familiar. They had been reinforced multiple times in my life. Now it felt true that Emmanuel was with me and that he cared about me.

I had very little memory of my time in Bowral. It was not the last time I would visit memories I had suppressed of the boys' home. Nor was it the only time I visited the womb. There were other things to see, but not yet. This was enough for now.

∼

I was still a bit shaken when I gingerly edged the Roller away from the fence and carefully turned her around to face the right way.

The others piled back into the car, and we headed off again.

"We're getting into some steeper track now, a lot more winding than it has been. It also gets pretty slick when it's wet so don't be in too much of a hurry to get out of second gear. That will also give you time to have a look around. The view is magnificent as we get up a bit." I nodded my head. Somehow, I knew Emmanuel wasn't just talking about my driving.

"Second gear is quite powerful. It has lots of pull. You can do a lot with it, pulling a load and climbing. You have time to pick your line, to point the car where it needs to go. It's more strength than speed, but it gives you time to exercise caution, to negotiate the best tack, to plan what you're going to do. Sure, you're not flying high, but make no mistake about it: here we come!

It's not like first gear, just starting. You are on your way and getting somewhere. Second gear has its limitations but it's still a fun gear. Second is a gear of caution, but you have your head above water. Then, you pick another gear, and you go faster. Don't try to fly before your wings develop and grow." He grinned at me. "They are growing, you know".

I grinned back, taking in what he was telling me. As I said, it had nothing to do with the gear box.

We started the pull up the hill, negotiating the corners much more comfortably. After driving for some time, I saw a lookout sign, and we pulled over to gaze out at the vista. It felt good to stretch our legs. We could see the city we had left behind in the distance. The sounds of the night were beginning to stir as the kookaburras gave their last burst of laughter before calling it a day.

It was such a peaceful time of day, just as the last of the sunset began to fade. Most of its glory was lost behind the mountains as it faded, but the glow had spread to colour every cloud with splendour as far as the eye could see. Now, the lights of the city we had left behind could be seen more clearly. All the city hustle and bustle disappeared from this distance.

"It's stunning," I said, as Emmanuel came across to where I was leaning against the lookout railing.

"Yes, it is," He agreed, putting his arm around my shoulder. We stood for a while taking it in.

"Would you like some soup?" Even as he said the words the fragrance of the goulash invaded my senses, pulling me away from the view.

I have no idea how he did it, but boy, it was good! Thick hearty soup in the best Hungarian tradition served with big chunks of crusty bread slathered in butter. Yum! I love good food. The variety of flavours from around the world is amazing. I just love good food!

This was what my wife called 'the ministry of the interior' and it was working a treat. Slowly my jangled nerves unwound.

We stood there, all of us together, eating the warming soup and enjoying the easy banter. This was good. The young Mechanic, Commander, Scarecrow, and Clown, all the parts of me, we were together. We belonged together. Without anything being said, somehow, I knew it was time.

Emmanuel spoke to each part in turn and then gently drew us and we merged into one, these parts of me absorbed into the person that I am, enriching and expanding my capacity. I felt a sense of joy, of wholeness, of completeness. It felt so right.

Chapter Twelve

I was strangely tired for a couple of days before my life returned to normal, if living life in the middle of a renovation can ever be called normal. The plasterboard installers had put up new wall sheets that needed to be painted and the electrician had been installing downlights. There were clouds of new dust generated in the process.

Each new phase bought its own challenges; long days, hard physical work, problem solving, keeping ahead of trades people, making decisions—lots of decisions. What we had visualized for a tired old house was taking shape before our eyes. It was very satisfying.

∼

A bunch of mates had planned a camping trip for the Easter long weekend and invited me to come. Absolutely! I jumped at the idea. A bit of a break, even for a few days, sounded very appealing. I had no idea that the recent changes would be tested.

CALEB

Several of my mates had left early, in time to be there before dark. I had needed to finish painting the living room ceiling before I could leave so it would be ready for yet more downlights. I didn't want to stall the electrician when he returned after the long weekend. They were hard enough to get on site without holding them up.

Sarah helped me throw my things together so I could pack my vehicle for the trip. She was looking forward to some alone time, her best idea for a break.

I made the last part of the journey after dark, well aware of the wombats and kangaroos that frequented our lonely, country roads.

I had been to this place on numerous occasions. The camp was on private property owned by one of the guys, land too rugged to graze sheep, now set aside for recreation. Any labour was strictly for enhancing our fun. Over time, all sorts of necessities made their way down there. On previous visits, we had built a shelter against the cooler nights, a big shed closed off on three sides but open to the sunny north. Different people had brought along a barbeque or two, someone else a table and chairs. There was even an old kitchen sink. We had made it quite comfortable in a rustic, blokey sort of way. Days were spent bush walking, four-wheel driving, fishing, and enjoying the great Aussie outdoors. Evenings were whiled away around the campfire, telling yarns, eating camp oven roasts, and indulging in a beer or two. Good mates, good food and good fun.

Our campsite overlooked a creek that had been overrun by prospectors during the gold rush. They had invaded this part of the Blue Mountains of New South Wales from every corner of the globe, as they had so many other parts of Australia. Then it would have been a long arduous trek on foot or horseback through the rugged and inhospitable terrain. Evidence of their industry still remained, overgrown and forgotten. The bush had long since reclaimed the mounds created with back-breaking labour in the hope of striking it rich. There had been enough gold in the creek to lure a syndicate to drag in a steam-driven stamper to break up the rock. Its loud pounding would have dominated the once quiet valley, but that had also grown still and was rusting into oblivion.

The magnificent sweep of the Milky Way had been unobstructed above me as I left my driveway, but several kilometres from my destination, I drove into rain.

We accessed the property through a neighbouring farm—six kilometres of narrow, roughly formed dirt track, some of it cut out of the side of the mountain. There was also a second, less steep, but far longer track. I felt well prepared, so I chose the shorter route we normally took.

The lumpy tyres that had sung to me while I was on the tar were now coming into their own. The gearing, built for just such terrain was perfect for the steep track. Slow and steady, and in low range when I needed it, I traversed the familiar trail.

The track was mostly rocky and firm until I came to the steep pinch near the crest. I only had to climb to the top and then weave my way down to the creek to make it to the campsite, but the rain had softened the ground making it extremely slippery. The vehicles that had preceded me to camp earlier that day had churned up the surface. My treads filled with the thick mire and the tyres quickly became as slick as the track. I could feel myself losing traction, the big 4x4 wallowing drunkenly. *This was not good.*

I stopped.

Try again. I carefully eased her forward.

The vehicle skewed sideways, the big wheels screwing me towards the precipice.

STOP!

I pulled out the torch I always kept close at hand and swivelled the beam to assess the situation.

Not good. Really not good!

Pouring rain—dark, sheer drop, back wheel centimetres from the edge…

Okay. Try backwards. Opposite lock. Gently does it.

Nup! It's not allowing me to steer!

My rear wheel was now balanced precariously right on the very edge of the drop. If I tried that again…

Stop—take a breath—assess.

I sat there, mentally running through my options. What options?!

I prayed.

Somehow, I *had* to get away from the edge, so I could either take another run at it or else go back and then around the long way. I had passed the alternative route about half-way from the main gate.

Again, I mentally checked the equipment. *Ropes, snatch strap, tow strap—I need both hands—head lamp, UHF radio…*

I was still running through the list in my head when I felt her slip. My heart jumped up into my mouth. The weight of the vehicle on the steep slope and greasy surface was enough. If I didn't do something I would find myself careering over the edge. It was a long way to the bottom—a very, very long way.

Oh God! What am I going to do now?

First things first! Tie her off.

It was becoming obvious that I wasn't going to be able to drive my way out of this one. I groped for my head lamp as I clambered over the gear stick to exit through the passenger door. The steep face of the cut-in met me, a wall created when the track had been carved into the side of the mountain. I clung to the car on the greasy surface as I searched for the sturdy rope I had thrown in at the last minute.

It's okay to have a rope, but what do I tie it to?!

A substantial tree root protruding from the bank looked promising. *I sure hope it's strong enough.*

Driving rain made every move cumbersome and my fingers fumbled with the wet rope as I secured the front of the 4X4 to the tree root. I was trusting my life and my truck to an old rope and a precarious-looking, twisted root.

Okay, now what?

I clambered through the passenger door out of the rain. I was soaked to the bone. Little rivulets ran from my clothing to join the mess of mud I was leaving on the floor. I tried the UHF radio hoping I would have reception. No response. Darn!

As I contemplated my next move, I became aware of Emmanuel with me. I couldn't see him like I did in the Roller, but I was aware of him.

"Emmanuel, I need your wisdom mate." Yep, he was definitely there.

There was a slight bend in the track. *I wonder—would the straps be long enough?* A plan was beginning to form in my head; a bit harebrained but maybe… Somehow, I had to get the rear end of the truck back onto the track. I had to get that wheel away from the edge!

I crawled out again, spreading more mud. The beam of my torch scanned the hill above the cut-in. Not much in the way of trees. Mostly, there were only young saplings but—one tree, forward of the truck. Would the straps reach?

There was only one way to find out. I was banking on the slick surface allowing the vehicle to slide, this time towards the bank, and safety.

I pulled the straps from the back floor, grateful that they were within reach, and began the painfully slow task. Groping for handholds, a rock here, a sapling, a root, I hauled myself up the bank onto the steep slope and made my way towards the tree. *Find an anchor point—wedge myself—haul the equipment—find the next anchor point—haul again.* The incessant rain hampered every move, running across my eyes and impeding my vision.

I wound one strap firmly around the trunk and attached the second one to the first. *Back down the slope—tie off the vehicle. If I say it really quickly, it sounds easy.*

The miracle was: it reached—just.

I used a large stick to wind up the slack, making the straps as taut as possible, pushing the end of the stick into the ground to stop it unwinding. I had no margin for error. If the straps gave, if any single thing failed…

Now for the test.

I contorted my body once again across the console to reach the driver's seat. The mud I was spreading in the car was now the least of my concerns. The hair stood up on the back of my neck as I gingerly took her out of gear, released the handbrake and slowly lifted my foot off the brake.

It worked! Yes, it worked!!!

Like something out of a textbook. It worked!

The arc of the straps, the slope of the road, the slippery surface and the weight of the vehicle all cooperated perfectly to pull me away from the edge. I slid gently sideways and backwards about two metres before I felt the wheels drop into the ruts that would ferry me out. The straps had held, the tree was perfectly positioned, and I had done it!

I sat for some time, just breathing, before going back out into the wet night to retrieve the equipment. Unceremoniously dumping the sorry mess of muddy, tangled equipment into the back, I once more climbed in behind the wheel.

I needed to reverse down the track about 400 metres before I could turn around, cautiously hugging the side of the mountain. The idea of attempting another run at that pinch had long since been jettisoned. *Not tonight baby, no way.* I had to take the long way around.

"Thanks Mate. I appreciate your help. I really needed it."

∼

I was several hours late when I finally rolled into camp wet, muddy, scratched up, exhausted, but triumphant.

"What happened to you?!" Dave, one of the guys, threw the question at me. Four sets of eyes were trained on me. I was a mess and so was my vehicle.

The story of my escapade had to be told. As I described where I had been stuck their eyes widened.

"How did you get out of that?"

There was no getting round it—not that I wished to. They wanted all the details. It was so good to see my mates. They had expected me hours before and they were aware of the treacherous conditions. They knew how dangerous it had become that night and had been wondering where I was.

I cleaned up the worst of the muck, changed into dry clothes and filled my belly with the tucker the boys had left over from their barbeque. I finally crawled into my swag. It was the only sort of crawling I had left in me. I had had my fair share that night. The rain had stopped, and a handful of stars glimmered overhead before I closed my eyes wearily. Tomorrow would be a better day.

It gave me a fresh appreciation for those intrepid gold miners of so many years ago, toiling in the hope of finding that precious metal. They would have faced perils almost every day. My musing didn't last long as my tensed muscles relaxed into sleep.

∽

It was as I was waking up the next morning that Emmanuel showed me his perspective of my little escapade. He had personally taken charge of the whole situation. There had been angels all around my vehicle. They had stopped me slipping over the brink and had helped me at every turn. I had everything I needed: the clarity of thinking, the clever idea, the right gear, one tree in exactly the right spot. Even before I left home, it had started: the new batteries in the headlamp, throwing in that old rope, there was so much.

It wasn't luck. Not at all! Wow!

I felt his affirmation. "You did very well back there, Caleb." It warmed me and set the tone for a wonderful weekend.

"Thank you! So did you," I grinned in reply.

I felt completely chuffed over the whole experience.

CALEB

Chapter Thirteen

Hot running water is such a luxury. Not that I could smell myself. I knew I would be confronted with the stink in the morning when I sorted out the mess, I had thrown in the back of the 4x4. It could wait 'til then.

I had come home late on Monday afternoon from the camping trip and had only stopped to shower and change before we sat down for the meal that Sarah had prepared.

"How was your trip?" I knew the question would be coming and I took a deep breath and launched in.

Her eyes widened, and her face blanched as I told her about my weekend.

"Oh, my. You could have died, Caleb!"

"I know. It was close. Too close," I admitted.

"I'm so glad you're okay." She reached out her hand and I took it.

"Me too."

Having such a close call made me acutely aware of how very much I appreciated her and how much I needed her.

"I love you."

"I love you too." We sat for a long time before the moment was broken by the awareness of our cooling meal.

It was a couple of weeks later that I was sitting in the living room in front of the heater. I love the glorious autumn days with trees ablaze with colour against azure blue skies, perfect weather for a bit of hard work. Evenings were cool enough to begin lighting the fire.

I sat in my lounge, no longer swathed in dust sheets, with a mug of coffee in my hand. It was such a good feeling to be pleasantly tired from a good day's work and to be able to relax in my own place. I was pleased with what we had achieved. I could look around and see the result of my labour: freshly painted walls, crisp white timber work, and the furniture finally in place. The colours Sarah had chosen looked great.

She had retired earlier while I lingered, waiting to reload the fire for the night. As I sat, staring into the flames, my mind began to wander.

Is this what I am meant to be doing? I could so easily have lost my life. How would Sarah cope if that had happened?

I could find no answers.

My mind turned to my dad and to our relationship. My attitude towards him had changed a lot, but I still had questions. My musing continued for some time, and I realized I wanted to talk to Emmanuel about it. It wasn't like I was triggered; I just wanted to be with him. I was so grateful for his friendship and for what he had done for me. He was everything my father had not been able to be. As I started to talk to him, I found myself back in the Roller.

She was winding through some exquisite country. The vegetation had changed as we climbed higher. We still had a long way to go before we reached the highest peaks, but we had left the cleared, agricultural land and now the forest, tall and thick, towered around us. The clouds dump their load as they encounter the mountain ridges, keeping the vegetation lush and green. The delicate fern fronds graced the narrow spaces between the towering eucalyptus trees. Broken sunlight filtered through the canopy, flickering across the road in a dancing lightshow as we passed.

The familiar sound of the elusive whipbird resonated through the dense undergrowth, and moments later a lyrebird startled me, darting across in front of us, his remarkable tail trailing. It was impossible to tell whether the sound had come from the master mimic or from a real whipbird. Echoing answers rang out from deeper in the bush. We had passed a messy mound of leaf litter a little way back, probably the site of the impressive courtship dance for which the lyrebird is so famous. It was a rare treat to see him, even on a minor road such as this.

There must be hardly any traffic on this track, I mused.

I had only seen one lyrebird in the wild before, miles from anywhere. It was only the unexpected sound of a car alarm deep in the bush that had alerted me to his presence. He expertly imitated the sound of the car alarm, a chainsaw, and an extensive repertoire of bird songs. He really was amazing.

Emmanuel was relaxed and obviously enjoying himself. He sat beside me in the luxurious leather seat, as the Roller purred in pure contentment. It also seemed to be enjoying our drive. It was much quieter now. Having only two of us in the car made dialogue much easier.

Our conversation drifted here and there until, finally, I raised the subject that had been on my mind: my father. I had often been told how much I was like him in both personality and appearance. People had expected me to *be* him in some way, to pursue the same goals, to share the same passions and specially to take on the farm when he retired. I knew that it had been my Father's hope.

"You are not your dad, you know. You were never meant to be. You are like your dad, yes, but you are not him."

"I think I've felt that I should be more like him, especially around the farm. I know he was disappointed when I didn't want to take that on." I had left home as soon as I had the opportunity, not looking back.

"And he did really well with share trading," I continued. "I don't understand why it hasn't worked for me." Back then it all happened more slowly, using a broker to make recommendations and to place the trades. Dad had studied different companies thoroughly, placing long-term trades. Now everything happened so fast with the internet allowing real-time access to the trading floor.

"Sure it's worked. Just not to make you heaps of money." He grinned, taking any sting out of the words. "That's what you have been learning, to be yourself, the person you were always created to be. When people are themselves, they enjoy life so much more."

"Yeh, I guess."

"When you get to the top of the hill there is a turn-in. If you pull over, I want to show you something."

"Okay."

Sure enough, there it was. I eased the big car to a stop and we both got out.

Emmanuel didn't open the door. He just stepped out and stood up! I stared at him. Did that just happen?

"One day you will be able to do that too." He was enjoying his own joke.

"Really?"

"Yes, really." Maybe he wasn't joking. Seriously? Oh boy, he unbalances me at times.

He indicated an opening through the bushes and together we headed towards it. As we did, I transformed into a young child, and I reached up to hold Emmanuel's hand. We stepped through the opening and into another realm. Just like that. There was no fuss, no fireworks. We just stepped in.

You know the term 'out of this world'? Yeh, well it fits. All the splendour of the magnificent high country we had just been enjoying felt like a faded old sepia photo in comparison.

"Is this Heaven?" My eyes were big as saucers as I swivelled my head to look at the breathtaking wonders.

"Yes, it's a part of it. It's a pretty big place. This is just one little corner."

"Wow! It's awesome!"

Words like verdant, beautiful, superb, and astonishing' any superlatives, were understated in this place. Fruit trees hung heavy with fruit I didn't recognise, and flowers nodded in colours I could not begin to describe. Everywhere I looked was awe-inspiring.

We were moving down a manicured, grassy slope towards a large city. The city drew me towards it but, for some reason, I found myself craning around looking back the way we had come.

There was something I didn't want to leave behind, tugging at my heartstrings. Something that was being destroyed on the other side of the rise, and I wanted to rescue it. I could feel the reluctance and anxiety of looking back whenever I turned my head in that direction. When I looked towards the city, I was peaceful. That was the way Emmanuel wanted to head, but it didn't seem as exciting as what was behind me. I was in a quandary. It didn't make sense. Going his way was steady and sure. I got the idea it was a much more fruitful way, a more positive way. Back the other way seemed to offer excitement, a sense of achievement, of something I could do myself. It seemed to have better chances, but I also understood that it was an illusion.

I was only pint-sized and like a parent, he picked me up to keep me moving in the right direction. My arm slipped around his neck and my thumb into my mouth as I continued to take in the scene as he walked. It settled me and I was able to stop looking backwards. I felt completely safe in his arms.

CALEB

He seemed to understand my chatter despite the thumb, smiling and responding. After a bit I wanted to get down.

"I want to walk myself."

"Okay, you're big enough to walk, but you need to stay with me." He again held my hand, matching his steps to my little ones.

As we walked, I grew a bit, but I was still small enough that he needed to hold my hand.

The city we were heading towards was on the other side of a crystal-clear river. Even from a distance the sandy bottom was discernible. We had to cross over a bridge to reach the main gates. People of every nationality were coming and going. They could come and go as they pleased here. The gates were always open. They could go on either side of the river. There was nothing to hold them here. They chose to be here.

Somehow, I knew that this was Emmanuel's place, the place where he *is*.

We walked together through the ornate gates, Emmanuel still holding my hand.

We stopped just inside the gates. I got the idea that there was a lot more to see but that I was here to just have a peek, a little glimpse of this amazing place. The streets were gold! There were jewels and gold everywhere, piles of them, treasure in every direction.

The people who live here just have it, they have it all. It never runs out. It's not like they each have their own. It's all there for everyone. They share it. There is far more than they need and they can use it any time they want it. Nobody seems to work all that hard, they just enjoy what's there. They have the whole valley. Some of them are picking flowers or fruit. It's all here. If only it was like this on earth.

I was awestruck by what I saw.

"Can I live like this?"

"You certainly can."

"How?"

"You just have to be here. I will lead you, you just have to follow," was his enigmatic reply.

⁂

Suddenly we were back at the Roller, and I was an adult again. We sat together on the wide running board.

For some reason I still wasn't happy. I was filled with conflict. A jumble of thoughts and emotions surfaced as if exposed by what I had just experienced.

"That's great," I blurted, "but I still want to go it on my own. What I find fulfilling is being able to achieve it. It's not so much about having it as achieving it. It's about what I can do: like I am clever, capable, important, and able to do stuff. I think that's why I love to design and make things. It's a huge part of my motivation, my drive. I'd feel useless or worthless if I didn't have that." Emmanuel listened quietly as I vented.

"I feel a whole lot better about gaining something myself rather than having it given to me. I think I despise having to be given to, needing a handout." As I said it, I could feel how hollow it sounded. All my efforts to be someone and all my achievements were like dust blown away in the wind leaving no evidence that they had ever existed.

He was showing me all this and I still wanted dust?

"Emmanuel, I need your help. I don't get it."

"When we work together, even in the everyday things, they can be gold, a bit of heaven on earth. The things you can achieve on your own are earthbound and they will all be dust one day, every single one." He responded.

"When I'm here with you I can see it a bit better, but I lose it so easily."

"I want to teach you how to live out of this place, the place where I am. Then you will learn how to receive, not just take. You have a part to play but you don't have to figure it all out yourself. Even that is a gift. I know what you need. As you can see there is an abundance to go around."

"Why do I lose the plot so easily? I just forget what we have been talking about. It doesn't feel real in the day to day. I get bogged down and I forget." I was sobered by the thought of just how easy forgetting seemed to be. A taste of something amazing had been given to me and I didn't want it to slip through my fingers.

"Yes, it is easy for you to forget. It will take some practice. Heaven is more real than all the things that you can touch and feel, all the things that are tangible to your five senses.

Your life has created a grid for you, an expectation of what life should be. You have built your life around that grid. It's time for a new grid. Every time you hang out with me, part of that old grid gets broken down and a new one gets built, one that is built on the dream Papa has for you. It fits you so much better than your own dad's dream or anyone else's either, including your own."

"Is that why I hang on to the dust? Is that about my grid?"

"Ah, hah! As you discover Papa's dream, you will find that it resonates with the deepest part of you. It is the most wonderful, fulfilling thing to live that dream.

Your father's shoes are far too small for you. This way you end up like your true Father." he grinned his now familiar smile, "My Dad."

"Your dad did the best that he knew how. He had his own damage and with the mischief of the enemy as well… Yep, that's what we are working on."

"So how do I do this, living out of heaven?"

"That's what I have been showing you. It's the other part of the journey, learning to live out of me, out of who I am. Heaven is where I am."

At that, I found myself back in my comfortable lounge chair in my own home. The fire had died down to a few glowing embers. It was too late to resurrect it now. I sat staring into the dark red glow for some time mulling over what Emmanuel had said.

The house was dark except for a lamp Sarah had left burning when she had retired. I yawned as I stood to place the cup in the dishwasher and follow her to bed.

I had a lot to think about.

CALEB

Chapter Fourteen

"Honey."

"Hmmm?" The coffee mug I was vacantly perusing captured the little attention I could muster.

"I need to talk to you," Sarah tried again, eggs in one hand and pan in the other.

"What is it?" I took another swig of coffee hoping it would help wake me up a bit. Winter always made it a bit harder to roll out of bed, and I was never at my best first thing in the morning.

"You know I caught up with Tina yesterday?"

"Hmmm." I nodded, rousing slightly.

"She is in all sorts of trouble. She is up to her eyeballs in debt and her eldest, Madeline, has started self-harming again. I told you already that her ex-husband has hidden all his assets in his company? Everything else is in his new wife's name. Jack has weaselled his way out of paying maintenance for the 4 kids! He doesn't pay a cent! That is not right! Just to put the icing on

CALEB

the cake he left last week for a six-week European holiday! I think that's what has set Madeline off again. Tina will lose her job if she takes any more time off. Darn! I thought he was better than that!" The eggs were being briskly whipped into submission.

"So did I. He seemed like a decent sort of bloke." We had known them socially for some years and had watched their lives unravel over time.

I was awake by now and I unwound out of my chair to make the toast.

Sarah continued, spatula waving, punctuating her rising passion. I knew much of the story already, a complicated tale of betrayal, infidelity, divorce and lies, all the ugly distressing blows that had left this little family battered and broken.

"What are you thinking? How can we help?" I already knew the answer even as I said it. Platitudes would do nothing. Tina needed money, cold hard cash. We weren't exactly rolling in it ourselves.

"Can you find out how much she needs?" I asked.

What she discovered was that doctor's, solicitor's and utility bills had mounted up over time until they came close to $10,000. I wrote out the cheques. Sarah did the leg work. We got it done. Sarah was delighted but I felt hollow inside, like it was an obligation, a chore, a duty, anything but a delight.

Jack! What was the man thinking? It should be an easy decision man! Don't go overseas this year. They are your kids!

This whole thing had got under my skin, but I knew I could ask for help, that I could talk to Emmanuel about it.

The Roller hadn't moved from the last time. We were parked by the side of the road in the same spot where we had stopped before, near the gap in the bushes.

I had hardly greeted Emmanuel before I vented about Tina and Jack and those bills, and about some of my own bills. "Why am I the one bailing people out? I'm not exactly flush! The trading hasn't been flying. This is just costing us! How am I ever going to make that money back?" Emmanuel let me rant.

"I'll never see that money again! I might as well throw it away. It's easy to give it out but I will never get it back—it feels like that anyway." I petered out, feeling the pain hiding underneath.

Gently, he prodded until I was able to see how much I believed that it was all up to me; that I had to look after myself; that nobody else would. It was a lonely, very stuck place.

"How do I get out of this bind? What do I do?"

"Money is not your security. If the winds pick up, it can all be blown away. If you hang onto me, you will still be okay, even if everything in your life were to go. I can help you with this. You're not on your own." Emmanuel's reassurance was palpable as we sat together in the front of the Roller.

He reached out his hand and I grabbed it with both of mine. Could he really help me if it came to that?

I was picturing myself being battered in a storm, soaked to the bone, my clothes plastered against my body, bits and pieces of my life swept away around me, but I still clung to him. *I've got to keep hanging on.*

They were sobering thoughts. I let his words wash over me.

Money isn't bad, a bit fickle but not bad in itself. I had certainly experienced that. It's about where my security lies. That's the issue. I remembered the vision I had of heaven. There had been an endless supply there. *Is that what he is talking about?*

"Papa has everything you need." I still clung to his hand as he spoke. "Giving is not about what leaves your hand. It's about what comes from your heart."

It seems like that is what this whole journey is about—my heart.

CALEB

It was weeks later that I awoke to the sound of rain. Fantastic! Maybe this time it would set in and deliver enough to break the seemingly endless drought. We were in what they call a 'green drought' in our district; enough rain to keep the grass looking okay but that was about all. The waterways were mostly empty and desperately in need of a good flush-out and the trees were languishing or dying. We were very fortunate compared to most of our sunburnt country. We at least had some grass left. Severe water restrictions were in place. Sarah and I had spent many hours hand-watering to save what we could. There was no vegetable garden again this year. The showers petered out that afternoon. A few days later we had a bit more. Not enough to break the long dry but so refreshing.

A week or so later I noticed some cracks in our home. They weren't all that big, but I was sure they had not been there before. My carpenter, who had only been available intermittently, was off on a jaunt overseas. We were also waiting for our kitchen. It had been ordered months ago and now it was holding up the work.

When a friend of mine, who had a handyman business, offered me a job I decided to take the opportunity. It would be good to have a bit of money coming in, but it kept my focus elsewhere. The house would have to wait. All our impetus ground to a halt. I was beginning to wonder if I would ever get the house finished.

Those cracks kept nagging at me. I was sure they were growing. They nibbled away at my confidence, eroding my resolve. *Had I done all this work just to have it crack up?* Inertia began to creep into my bones.

I filled my days working long hours and whiled away my evenings watching drivel on the box. I did a bit of trading and, for the most part, I broke even—no big losses, no big wins. On the weekends I retreated to my shed, tinkering with whatever I found to distract myself. I didn't seem to have the motivation to tackle anything major, just little nothing jobs.

I usually love creating and working on some projects in my shed, but I was disillusioned with every idea I came up with and I ignored the list of jobs I had to do on the house. The thought of them was thoroughly uninspiring. They weren't the only thing I was ignoring.

As weeks turned into months it seemed like everything in my life had seeped into tedium and struggle, leaving the colour and majesty of my experience with Emmanuel feeling like an unlikely delusion. Everything felt like it was hard, just—so—hard. Sarah tried to reach out to me, tried to draw me out, but I wasn't exactly responsive. I was ignoring her too.

When I finally got around to talking to Emmanuel about it, I found myself back on the running board of the Rolls Royce in exactly the same spot as before.

As I sat there, dejected, and absorbed in my own thoughts, I realized that the very thing I had told myself I wouldn't do, I had done. I had forgotten. All the things he had told me: to ask him for help, my encounter in heaven. I had forgotten.

"See these blocks?" Emmanuel interrupted my reverie to point out a heap of toy building blocks that had appeared on the grassy bank. The bottom few layers of a building were in place already.

"You just have to keep putting one block on top of another, one at a time." As he said it he continued building, one block at a time. "There are times when it feels like nothing has been happening. That's when you're just looking at the pile of blocks. When you look at what hasn't happened yet and the things that don't look like they are working, you lose your perspective. That's when disappointment and discouragement creep in."

"You mean 20,000 bricks don't make a house unless they are laid," I said, without any enthusiasm.

"Yes, that's right. It's only one at a time but with each one a bit more of the building goes up."

CALEB

Absentmindedly I joined him, haphazardly placing blocks. Any plan or design was unclear to me, but as I followed his lead, a pattern was developing. It seemed completely random, but the beginnings of a house were emerging as we continued.

Yep, he was right. I had lost direction and all forward momentum by focusing on the problems. That's when I had forgotten what he had told me.

"You just keep doing the block thing, plodding along, one block at a time." he continued. "You forgot to come to me; you didn't ask me to help you. Why do you just include me in the things you find difficult? Why not in everything? I'd like that. That's a true partnership."

I knew it was a rebuke, but I didn't feel like I was being put down or shamed by his words or tone. I had never given it a single thought before. Maybe I was using him like a dentist or a doctor, someone I saw when the pain got bad.

If I only include him when I get stuck, I am using him! The thought struck me like a blow. I'd need to mull that one over some more.

"I don't know why I do that," I admitted. "I guess I hadn't really thought that you would be interested…" My voice trailed off. "My life is pretty boring really."

So much of my life is routine and monotonous. Maybe he would like to be with someone more interesting but with me? Why would he want to?

I looked across at him. He handed me a mug brimming with hot cocoa and sat quietly allowing me to continue my pondering.

I began to consider the journey we had been taking together, the amazing things that had happened. Like a clandestine double life, it had been anything but boring. Every time I was with this man it was amazing. I remembered what he had said about the gold of heaven becoming part of my every day. *Could it be?* "When we work together, even in the everyday things, they can be gold, like a bit of heaven on earth." That's what he had said.

Absentmindedly, I took a sip of the now cooling drink. I tend to put everything in compartments. Emmanuel was in a compartment for when things weren't going well. Sarah was in another one. Work, friends, responsibilities—yep, all very neatly boxed. This guy was consistently challenging my boxes, and sometimes blowing them apart! Maybe I'd be better off without them…

The building blocks he was on about, that's not just the routine of everyday, like push-through-and-get-on-with-your-chores. It's about relationship. That's what the building is about!

"That's it isn't it?" I burst out. Anyone else would have wondered what on earth I was talking about, but this guy knew my thoughts. He knew!

"That's it exactly. I love hanging out with you."

He wants to do life with me. It's something you buy into, more like a marriage than a friendship. I had lots to think about, but I knew it was something that I also wanted.

It was time to head out, get back in the big car and get on our way.

"Let's do it," I said with more enthusiasm than I had felt in a while.

With a grin, Emmanuel joined me as we left the little patch of sunshine we had been sitting in. We piled into the car and resumed our journey. The little pile of blocks vanished as we did so, their object lesson completed.

The trees were gradually becoming smaller and more stunted as we climbed higher. The towering alpine ash had given way to the beautiful snow gum, hardy survivor of the cold and unforgiving winds of the long months of winter, when snow covers the ground. Ribbons of bark expose amazing hues of blue, green, deep red and orange on the twisted gnarled trunks in spring. The tones soften in the frequent rain showers of summer to produce pure white, creams, soft greys, or greens.

We had seen several wallabies and wombats on the lower slopes but here the birds dominated. Often colourful and migratory, they take advantage of the warmer months to partake of the abundant feed on offer. Only the hardiest animals remain throughout the winter, those small enough to hide under the insulating snow and survive on the scant remaining food.

Years ago, the majestic mountains lured intrepid explorers, pioneers, and bushmen to conquer their enigmatic heights, already well-known to Australia's first people. The lush summer pastures brought settlers, timber men tackled the tall forests, and gold enticed adventurers to brave the isolation and danger of the mountain wilderness. Their exploits are the stuff of campfire yarns, folklore and legends that have inspired generations of poets and songsmiths. These brave men and women are part of the fabric that has made Australia what it is today.

The road had become little more than a dirt track, narrow and winding, with deep ruts and frequent wash-aways. It was the sort of place where one expected to see the warnings at the track head: "Check road and weather conditions before proceeding", "Four-wheel drive vehicles only", "Carry all appropriate recovery gear, maps, chainsaw" etcetera, etcetera. Deep shade and frequent rain kept some parts of the road perpetually wet. Natural springs and creek crossings were common. It was not only the early explorers who needed courage to traverse these parts.

We, however, were in a beautiful, early-edition Rolls Royce, a lot dirtier than when we had started out but surprisingly unscathed, despite our adventures thus far. Somehow, she had managed everything I had thrown at her without missing a beat. I had missed more than one beat, myself, navigating the difficult terrain. Mr Henry Royce, having won so many endurance races in his day, had created a machine worthy of the title of best car in the world. He tackled any flaw or weakness with dogged determination, resulting in a vehicle renowned for its reliability and engineering excellence.

I realized that we had seen very few travellers on the road, even when we were much closer to the city. Not for the first time I wondered about the wisdom of this venture. There were moments when I even questioned my sanity. We were taking a priceless vintage car through this?! What was I thinking? Even my 4 X 4 would find this challenging.

As we rounded a corner, the sparse, twisted snow gums abruptly gave way to alpine grassland. Now, only the odd, stunted, grotesquely contorted gum remained; the hardy ones that had found some shelter from the incessant winds. The shift was dramatic, and although we were still some way from the summit, a breathtaking panorama opened up.

A wide rest area beckoned us to stop a while. This view deserved to be savoured. Snow lingered in pockets where the sun couldn't venture, its rays unable to bring the temperature above single digits. I was very grateful for the warm clothing Emmanuel had provided when we first headed towards the mountains.

We found a bench seat thoughtfully placed to catch the sunshine and the view and sat down to another of Emmanuel's amazing feasts. This time it was minestrone, good hearty Italian, soul-warming soup with plenty of luscious, stinky parmesan on top. Yum. This was just what I needed—delicious, piping hot soup, served up here in this place miles away from anywhere. It was one of the many mysteries about this man. I had no clue where we were other than very close to the roof of Australia. I shook my head at the thought and continued to devour what was on offer. Amazing!

"Would you like to take a walk up to the top?" Emmanuel pointed to a winding track snaking towards the summit.

"Sure." The thought of stretching my legs was very appealing and the view from up there would be even more spectacular.

The path was steep and narrow and perpetually wet in places. The melted snow and the high rainfall sustained little streams and springs which filled the fens and bogs, supporting flowers unique to this wild, alpine area. Cheerful, yellow billy buttons nodded at us, and pretty, little snow daisies clothed large sweeps of the slope surrounded by the soft grey-green of their leaves. I knew the names of the buttercups and delicate little eyebrights, but there were many others whose names I didn't know. We stopped often to admire the beauty and to gaze into the fens. Large, rocky shelves gave shelter to tiny creeping plants and mosses.

We sat together on a rocky outcrop at the summit. A brisk breeze, icy cold, pulled at our clothing. I stared out over the view, uninterrupted in every direction, peak after peak still with remnants of snow in spots. It was, at once, exhilarating and totally peaceful. Every sense came alive, tasting the snow in the breeze, smelling the fragrance of the heath, hearing the trilling flow of water cascading over the rocks, the feel of the breeze on my face. An eagle arrested my attention for a long time, soaring effortlessly on the updraft created by the mountain. Everywhere was a feast for the eye. It was truly awe inspiring. We sat silently exalting in the beauty.

Finally, the warmth generated by climbing to the summit dissipated. Moisture had seeped through the fabric of my pants where I had been sitting, and the cuffs were covered in mud almost to the knees. It had taken a while but now the cold was undeniably making its presence felt, demanding attention. We watched the eagle spiral down to soar in the valley below us and then disappear from view.

"I could sit here forever but I'm getting a bit cold, so can we start heading down?"

"Even the eagle has to come down sometimes." Emmanuel stood up as he answered my question.

"Yeh, I guess so. They would get pretty hungry if they stayed up there forever."

Speaking out loud had broken the moment and we began our descent, gradually warming up again as we walked.

"The view from up here is amazing. I'm glad we came up here."

As we picked our way down the path the view of the road became clear, snaking into the distance in both directions.

"Gee, it's a bit rough!" I stopped, staring down at the road ahead. "Is that the way we are headed?"

"Sure. What are you concerned about?"

"Looks like there has been a bit of a landslide, and there's a really rough patch." I pointed in the direction of a very steep-looking pinch that was narrow and badly eroded. "That doesn't look real good."

"So, what is it you are concerned about?" He asked again, his gentle question halting me. What am I apprehensive about?

"I don't know. I just don't want to get stuck down there somewhere. If that is the little bit we can see, what is the rest of it like? It just doesn't seem safe. Maybe we should go back the way we came." I faltered to a halt.

"We have managed up until now."

"Yes, but…" My voice trailed off.

"But?"

"Isn't there an easier way?"

Although I was staring off in the direction of the road, I was no longer focused. Instead, I was seeing a pattern in my life. I had tended to avoid anything that I wasn't sure I could manage.

Even early in my high school days, I had worked out the system. If I didn't show up for sport on the first day of term, I wouldn't be on any of the teachers' attendance rolls and they wouldn't know I was missing. A couple of mates and I would regularly skip school on sports days. More than once a teacher had pulled up in traffic to yell across to us asking if we had a note from our parents excusing us. We had each pulled out a piece of paper from our pockets to wave in his direction before the traffic on the busy road began to move, forcing him to also move on. No one ever discovered our little ploy, and I escaped the boa constrictor of asthma and the indignity of losing out to much stronger boys. I was competitive, but only where I knew I could have a chance. Sport was not one of those areas. Cricket was okay. You didn't have to run so much. Running just knocked me up. That left pretty much every other arena of sport as something to be shunned.

CALEB

I tended to only do the things I was good at and didn't push into things I thought were too hard. Where did I decide not to put the effort in? That it's too hard, not worth it? Where did I feel like I have to short cut and not go the right way around, to only go for the things that would fall into my lap and not the things I have to work hard for?

"This is a fairly strong pattern in my life, isn't it?" I was aware that he knew my thoughts.

"Yes, it is."

Somewhere, I made a choice. I learnt not to push too hard. I told myself "Don't put yourself in that place; you will just get yourself knocked up. It's not worth it," I said.

Even during my apprenticeship, I hated the big jobs. I much preferred the smaller ones that could be finished in a day.

I have been great at getting things started but finishing has been a hassle. It's like I've got to do it in small amounts so I can manage it myself. Was it lack of capacity? I didn't know. The stamina hadn't been there to see things through, the endurance to push things to the conclusion.

"It's like I'm still expecting the asthma to bring everything to a grinding halt, still anticipating running out of breath. But I don't get asthma anymore. I hadn't since I was in my 20's. What is this? What is it I'm trying to get away from?" I asked him.

The memory or whatever it was came flooding in as I asked the question.

The sensation was like being in a washing machine, being battered about with no control. Thrashing—distressed—twisted up—tangled—trapped—aggravated. This is not how it should be…

The womb…

What?

I snapped out of the distressing memory with a jolt, shaken by the brief glimpse.

"Emmanuel, what was that?" I could hear the panic in my voice.

"It was the womb, like you thought."

"I don't ever want to go back there!"

"What's going to happen if you do?"

"It feels like I will be trapped forever, like being in the worst nightmare forever!" My whole body trembled, whether from the encroaching cold or the shock of the memory, I wasn't sure.

"I can't do it! I can't go back there! I'd be trapped—alone…" Just the thought of revisiting that memory felt completely overwhelming.

"It isn't as deep or as hard as it feels, and I would go with you. You don't ever have to do it alone." He reached out his hand and placed it over my wildly beating heart. Gradually the panic subsided.

"Now is not the time to look at that. We need to get you down to the car and into some dry clothes." His touch and matter of fact tone calmed the terrors.

I don't know how long we had been standing there on the path with me staring out, sightlessly, towards the horizon but I realized it was beginning to get late and we still had some way to go to reach the Roller.

We continued down the path. The light was fading as the sun dipped behind the elevated horizon. It spread a rosy glow and deep shadows over the unusual landscape.

As it grew darker, I realized that Emmanuel himself was glowing, illuminating the path ahead. His skin and clothes were light! Not as bright as to blind me, just enough that the path was safe and clear. Everything about this man—he never ceases to amaze me! It wasn't that he made everything easy; not at all. But having him with me—yes—he was with me. That's what makes the difference.

I concentrated on the path, attempting to avoid the deepest of the wet patches. It was a bit of a lost cause, my boots and lower legs had long since been saturated. Eventually the path levelled, and we crossed the road to the waiting Roller.

After changing into clean, dry clothes and boots, pulled from goodness knows where, I deposited the sodden mess I had been wearing into the trunk on the running board. I gratefully climbed into the car again. Gradually the warmth of a thick blanket, and the hot drink Emmanuel handed me, penetrated the cold recesses of my body, and my thoughts turned from my frozen toes to our recent conversation.

"How could I possibly remember when I was in the womb? It felt very real, but it is not very likely. Is it?"

"Sure, you remember. It's not like remembering what you had for breakfast, it's a different sort of memory, but it's just as real. These are things that have influenced you all your life."

"Really?"

"Uh-huh."

"I'm going to have to look at it sometime, aren't I?"

"If you want to be free from the influence of it, yes." I nodded, beginning to grasp the significance of the snippet of memory.

"How would it be if we had a look at the womb from a distance, without actually going there? That way we can sort through some things and break it down into more manageable pieces."

"Can we do that?"

"Yes, we can. When it is time to go to the memory, you can skip out at any time and I will help you regain your equilibrium. I will protect you. You don't have to do it all at once and you don't have to do it alone. In that place, you have very little capacity, and you will be feeling that. That's why we need to break it down. Your capacity will grow as you conquer each piece."

"Okay." In the safety of the car, the thought was not as daunting as it had been when standing on the windswept alpine moor.

Like a movie or a hologram, the story of my beginnings began to unfold in front of me. I could see my mother's fretfulness, the distress of a first-time mother who had no one to support her. My father, even more ignorant of the workings of pregnancy and childbirth than she, retreated to the safety of his work. Men were not welcome in that arena. It was not the done thing in that generation. The young mother was left on her own to comfort herself on her favourite sweets.

As she helped herself to another serving of dessert, I sensed the effect beginning. I watched as the baby retreated from the overstimulation, the effect of the dump of sugar.

Mum's blood pressure also soared dangerously, and the doctor's concern amplified her already heightened anxiety. I sensed the fear, not just in a passing thought but in a recurring torment. That's when I had started to thrash around, getting myself more and more tangled up.

It wasn't like that all the time. It seemed to come in waves. I had concluded that I needed to conserve my energy between the waves so I could survive. I never knew what was going to come down the tube next or when the next wave would hit.

There didn't seem to be any comfort or safety. I'm not even sure if there was any love and acceptance, either. Maybe it was there and just got blocked by the fear. I don't know. I couldn't feel Dad at all. He must have been there somewhere—but where?

Even though I was watching from a distance I could feel myself going numb.

"Caleb?" Emmanuel's voice called me back. "I think that's enough for now. You did very well"

"Thank you. That was hard." I was dazed by the encounter, but nowhere near as much as before.

"Yes, it is. Would you like to leave it with me, and I will soften it up a bit for you so it isn't so hard for next time?"

"Yes, please. That would be good." It was as if I had bundled the whole thing up and handed it across to him. I could feel warmth and safety slowly seep through my being, comforting me.

We sat for a time in companionable silence before Emmanuel pointed out into the darkness. In the distance I could make out city lights.

"That's our destination." It was beautiful, ethereal, and otherworldly. This was no ordinary city. It seemed to hover several ridges away towards the horizon, golden and glowing, enticing, drawing me towards it. I knew the road was rough and challenging but as I stared off into the distance, I knew that whatever was waiting for me in that place would be worth it, every bit of it.

"Not many people bother to go there. That's why there are so few people on the road, but it is well worth the effort," He said.

Right now, it was time to rest, but I knew, *I knew* I wanted to keep going.

The conversation drifted here and there aimlessly meandering into drowsiness and finally petering out into my snoring. I was unaware of Emmanuel watching me, gently tucking the thick blanket closer around my shoulders as I slept, dreamless and free from the distressing thoughts of the past few hours.

I woke in my own bed, rested, and refreshed.

Chapter Fifteen

Okay. The block thing he talked about—one at a time. What do I need to do first? I mused as I stood surveying the cracks, those infernal, tormenting cracks. They had grown since last time I looked. I was sure of it. Sarah joined me, two steaming cups of coffee in her hand.

"What are you thinking? Do we get the engineer?"

"I don't think so. Not yet anyway. I would like to try drainage first. I know that needs to happen in any case." I took an absent-minded sip of my drink. "Do you reckon this crack has grown?"

"I think so. That door into the front room doesn't shut properly anymore." It wasn't the only one either. I knew what was going to happen, whether the problem was fixed or not. It was going to cost, big time. I was now digging into the profit from the sale of our last house, something I had not wanted to do.

"It's nothing like the TV reno shows, is it? Buy, fix, flip and make a ton of money, right?" she said.

I couldn't help but smile. "Now that is an understatement." I chuckled wryly. "Flippin' heck more like."

"They make it look soooo easy." She gestured dramatically, before she paused and looked at me. "You'll get this, you know."

"Do you think? Sometimes I don't know."

"We may not make a heap of money on this if we sell. It's taken too long already, but you are going to conquer this. This house is going to be really classy when we are finished with it." She was totally serious now.

"Do you think? I hope so." Her words warmed me.

That same day I rang my mate Dave, one of the guys I go camping with, and also an expert earthmover. He is a busy boy, but he fitted me in and soon the ground around the back of the house, the driveway and the lawn were a mess. We put in rubble drains, pits and plumbing and then repaired the damage inflicted by the big machine. I sank thousands of dollars into the ground where no one would ever know the difference. A plasterer came and repaired the cornice and walls. I spent hours under the floor jacking and levelling until all the doors worked properly again. Sarah repainted the same cornice and walls—again.

I went through the motions, one step at a time.

It seemed to be working, until the next time it rained. Would it ever end?

God, I can't keep doing this. I just can't. What do I do? It was a silent prayer.

✼

The road was steep, little more than a track, narrow and with tight bends zigzagging carefully towards yet another summit. Enormous alpine ash majestically clothed the slopes, white trunks towering like regimented soldiers on parade. At this altitude, sudden storms can spring up unannounced, bearing down with the force of a freight train, dropping the temperature dramatically, and bringing snow even in summer, their unrelenting, offensive funnels through the gullies gathering momentum, mowing down even the strong.

Adrenaline raced as I locked up the brakes, skidding sideways to a halt. The Roller narrowly missed the massive girth that completely blocked the road. Recent rain had softened the soil and an enormous giant lay where it had fallen, a soldier taken in its prime, brought down by the malicious gale.

"How did we miss that?" My heart pounded painfully as if trying to escape my chest.

Emmanuel was completely unperturbed.

"Whew, that was fun!" He laughed out loud, delighted at the escapade.

I did not share his mirth.

"We could have been killed! Didn't you see that? There was no warning!" Irritation flashed, supplanting my fear.

"The angels had it under control. We are okay."

"It's all right for you! What are we going to do now? I bet you don't have a chainsaw in the back!"

"Caleb, it really is okay. None of this is too hard for me."

I slammed the door in agitation as I left the vehicle to survey the scene.

It was a giant ash. Where I stood in the middle of the road, the top side of the trunk was above my head. There was room for me to shimmy underneath if I crouched low, but there was no way known to get the vehicle through—no way, even if I folded down the windscreen and pulled down the canvas hood of the Roller. This was a monster of a tree.

To attempt to reverse back through the switchbacks far enough to turn around would be suicidal. I mentally navigated the course. No way; not an option.

As I stood there staring balefully up at my nemesis, I felt the familiar discouragement come crowding in. The numbness invaded, leaving me flat and defeated. We were trapped; utterly, completely trapped.

Quietly Emmanuel came to stand beside me. He handed me a mandarin, already peeled, and I ate it absentmindedly.

"It doesn't look good, does it?"

"No, it does not," I agreed darkly.

"We need to go back to the circus."

I turned from the obstacle in front of me to stare at the man. And I knew he was right.

∽

The circus—a place forever changed for me. Never again would it represent fun and adventure. Coming back was so hard.

I could see yet another part of me, a little boy—looking like a frozen statue—still standing in the ring where I had left him when I had made my escape from the clown. I could see in his eyes the nothingness, the blackness of the far reaches of space and the trauma. The clown had stolen from me—my innocence, my childhood, my dreams, my trust. He had left his mark on me. I'm damaged goods now—broken, no good, marred, forever tainted, totally humiliated. The shame of it had been branded into my soul—his mark, my shame—mutilating my personhood.

Irreparable—lost—rejected—hopeless. The laugh of the clown echoed around the big top—mocking, sneering, cruel. The sound of it had haunted my nights, invading my world, doggedly following me, ready to bring me down, reminding me of my worthlessness, my powerlessness.

See? It's no good! I'm hopeless. It's pointless trying. The contemptuous words went on and on. They had become my own. The familiar recording was seared into my brain, ready to repeat the litany of despair at any hint of danger.

I watched woodenly as Emmanuel hunkered down in front of the little one.

"It wasn't your fault." Gentle eyes gazed into my cold, blue ones.

"It was the clown. He did that to you. You didn't do anything wrong." The words were so simple but powerful. A tear escaped from the corner of the tiny statue's eye, just one. It ran down the stony face and Emmanuel caught it, carefully depositing it into a crystal bottle he had pulled from the pocket of his jacket.

I watched, mesmerized, as colour began to return to the sad little cheeks. Slowly it spread, life invading the darkness, truth evicting the lies. The clown who had been so brazen when we had arrived began to edge away, ashen faced. He had been found out, exposed. His mocking laugh no longer reverberated through the cavernous space. The only sound was Emmanuel's reassuring voice.

"You're okay now."

He reached out his hand, inviting the little one to take it. Timidly he did so, unsure still of his safety. The warm eyes and the soft voice melted the last of the reticence, and the little one melted into Emmanuel's healing embrace. It lasted for a long time with little arms wrapped tightly around Emmanuel's neck, hanging on for dear life.

He finally stood, lifting the little man up to survey the now empty arena. The transformation was complete.

"The bad man's gone!" Surprise filled the childish voice.

"Yes, he certainly has!"

They sat for a long time, the little one ensconced on the adult's knee, the safety of the hug allowing the little one and me to catch our breath and recover. It was as if everyone else just disappeared and we were alone. It was time to just be. Nothing else was needed—just be. This man was so easy to be with.

Very gradually, Emmanuel began to play with the little one. Toy cars appeared and they sat cross-legged, heads together making tracks in the sand and the obligatory brumming sounds. Cars have to make the right noise! Piggyback rides, chasings, and catching followed. Emmanuel had lots of time for a boy who had forgotten how to play. It took a while, but eventually, squeals of laughter came bubbling up like birds released from a cage to soar again.

CALEB

As I watched the shenanigans my heart responded, filling with hope and joy.

The tree was exactly where we had left it, firmly wedged in place. It was still 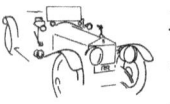 just as huge, still totally obstructing our path, but I was different. I grinned across at Emmanuel who was still eating a mandarin. Now this was interesting!

"So, what do we do?"

"Tell it to move out of the way."

"Really? Are you serious? Are you having a lend of me?"

"Really." He was smiling but I could tell that he meant it.

"He wants me to talk to a tree!" Suddenly, I burst out laughing at the absurdity of it all. Everything about this trip was unusual to say the least, so why not this? The whole thing tickled me, and once I started laughing, I couldn't stop. The noise echoed back across the valley resulting in fresh outbursts of mirth. I finally managed to control myself enough to catch my breath.

"Tree—ha, ha, ha, ha—move it!" I addressed the offending monster before, once again, exploding with belly laughter.

Emmanuel stood there, smiling but not at all surprised at my response or at what happened next.

Four of the biggest angels I could ever imagine appeared out of nowhere; big burly front row forward types, only upsized—I mean big-time upsized! They lifted that fallen giant as if it were a matchstick. Without fanfare, they hurled it over the edge of the steep bank. It meekly placed itself parallel to the track out of harm's way.

The road ahead was now clear.

With a flourish, the four of them bowed in unison, grinning like a bunch of schoolboys. They had obviously relished the opportunity. Just as quickly as they had come, they disappeared. I was left standing in the middle of the track, mouth gaping, thunderstruck at what had just happened.

Slowly, I turned to face my companion who shrugged his shoulders as if to say "See, I told you it wasn't hard."

Again, the gales of laughter escaped. This time, Emmanuel joined me, and it was some time before we could carry on an intelligent conversation, at least my part. It had been many years since I had laughed so hard. That felt so good.

Wow! What a day!

CALEB

Chapter Sixteen

When I finally came down a bit we began to talk about the renovation. He didn't tell me how to do it, but his encouragement really helped.

My perspective had shifted. It no longer felt like there was a whole panzer division bearing down on me. Hope began to course again, just a trickle, the flow that makes any venture seem conceivable. Maybe it wasn't impossible after all. Maybe…

Sarah told me later that there were several times she heard me chuckle in my sleep that night. She's an amazing woman; she actually believed me when I told her what had happened. I still shake my head when I think about it. The whole incident was extraordinary.

I began again. Everywhere I looked there were problems. That had not changed, but I set about looking for the little things I could do. They were small steps, but it was a beginning.

CALEB

~

Only a couple of nights later a dream startled me awake. "Urgh." The grunt escaped me into the predawn darkness.

"Are you okay?" Sarah's sleepy voice told me I had woken her.

"Yeh. Just a bad dream."

"Hmm. You were thrashing around a lot."

"Sorry."

I could hear her beside me, shifting position to try to recapture her disturbed sleep.

The dream shocked me with its intensity. Emotions it had generated lingered like the taste of gall on my tongue. I couldn't shake off the sensation.

"Sarah?" I quietly tested the darkness to see if she was still conscious.

"Hmm?" she mumbled, only just awake.

"Can I tell you about the dream I had? I think it's important, and I need your help, so I don't forget it."

"Hmm, sure. Just give me a sec…" Again, I heard her shift, this time to pull herself back from the brink.

"Thanks."

I slipped my arm around her, drawing comfort from her familiar presence.

"Okay. Shoot." She sounded a bit more alert now.

"In the dream, I was four-wheel driving with Paul Howard. Do you remember the guy I used to work with years ago?" Sarah mumbled her agreement.

"We had to take a diversion for some reason, so we ended up having to cross a creek and we got stuck. The water was up to the bonnet, and it was washing these things into the car."

"What sort of things?"

"Like worms." I shuddered at the recollection. "They were everywhere! I had to get out of there. I ended up sitting on the bank with worms attached to my feet. I pulled at them, and they kept coming and coming. I was pulling for ages to get them out. When I finally did, they left huge craters in my feet. There were heaps of them. When I looked, there were white insects in the craters eating my flesh."

"Yuk. That sounds gross."

"Yes. It was! I remembered that there was an ointment that would heal the mess and the next thing I knew I was on the nature strip on a busy road inside a sleeping bag. Those insect things were still eating my feet. I knew I was close to the house where they sold the ointment. I wasn't in any pain, but the white insects were sapping my strength. I managed to hail a guy coming out of the house. I asked him if his wife was at home because I knew she was the one who sold the ointment, but he was joking around, and I couldn't get his attention. I was obviously not in a good way, but he didn't seem to recognise that and kept fooling around, only giving me a fraction of his attention. I was weakening all the time. I knew that his wife had the ointment that would fix this, but I couldn't get through to him. There were people all around, but I couldn't get any help. There was no outcome, and then I woke up."

"That's awful! Do you remember anything else?"

"Yeh. When I was in the sleeping bag with those things eating away at my feet, I couldn't get out of the darn thing. I kept getting weaker and weaker. If I could just get out, then this guy would see the predicament I was in and know that I needed help, but I couldn't get out of the sleeping bag. Funny, the worms were only going for my feet."

"That must have felt horrible."

"It did. I've had a few dreams a bit like that recently, but I forget what they were. They leave me pretty flat when I wake up. I think it could be related to our finances. You know, the stuck feeling, being a bit overwhelmed? I guess I feel like the life is being sapped out of me. Every week, there is a bit less in the account. I'm not making the big losses anymore but we still aren't getting ahead."

"Yeh, I think you could be right."

We talked until the bird's enthusiastic welcome of a new day let us know it was too late to recapture any more sleep. Our own enthusiasm was a little jaded as we crawled out of bed. The dream had left me feeling mentally and emotionally flat.

∼

That evening I remembered the dream and the impact it had on me. I knew it must have some significance, especially when it left me feeling so flat.

I need to talk to Emmanuel about the dream.

I was finding that I could join Emmanuel in the Roller without having to have a trauma hitting me in the face. If I got to a quiet place without distractions, I just had to focus on Emmanuel, imagine myself there, and the vision would start again. It was a great way to hang out with him. I often did it in the evenings when the house was quiet, and the responsibilities of the day had lifted. It made me smile just thinking about him. I was so grateful for everything he had done for me.

∼

When I returned to the Roller, I was surprised to see that we had not made any progress since the last time. We were still parked in exactly the same spot. The big tree was still lying submissively down on the bank, but the Roller sat at an awkward angle across the road. It reminded me of the close encounter I had when I went camping that time. The angels had helped me then, and I guess they could do it now, but I had the idea there was more to this. Right now, I can't go forward, and I can't go backwards! It's not like I'm lost. I'm on the right track. The track is open, but I am stuck, facing the wrong way. The dream, the horrible worm things, the insects and being stuck in the sleeping bag—it was the same feeling.

"Emmanuel?"

"Yes?" He turned towards me.

"I had a dream the other night about these insects eating my flesh? Worms bored into my feet and made great big craters and they left insects behind. I'm wondering if that is somehow connected to—to everything?" I petered out.

"Not exactly. But it does affect you." He seemed to know all about the dream. "There is still something to look at back at the circus."

"Oh, no." I groaned at the thought.

"It's okay. Whenever you're ready."

I could feel anger rise in me at the thought of the incident at the circus and what the clown had done to me.

I thought again of the insects eating my flesh, the trapped feeling in the sleeping bag, unable to get help, then of our dwindling finances, and Sarah and the girls.

I sighed deeply with the realization of what I needed to do.

"I'm not going to get anywhere before I do, am I?" The thought of that made me angry too.

"No, mate. This is a pretty important one."

"Okay, let's do it." My teeth were clenched but the decision was made.

I could see the little one that was me marching towards the big steps that would take him back to his mum and dad. He was furious. His hands were balled into fists and his face contorted with anger. *That's a bad man!* The thought of the clown laughing at his expense, of everybody laughing, fuelled the fury. *He is getting away with it. It's not fair!* Anger at being betrayed, at being left alone and the injustice, grew with each step.

About halfway up the bleachers, Emmanuel called my name. The little one did not want to stop his headlong flight. There was determination in every stride as he negotiated the steps too big for his little legs, determination to get as far away as possible from that awful clown and never look back. To look back was to give that man another chance to hurt, to humiliate, to give him even more power. It would let that yucky clown off the hook and there was no way he wanted to do that.

Again, Emmanuel called my name, and this time the little one glanced across to see who it was. It took a bit but, finally, the little one realized that this was a friend, not someone who meant to harm him. This was not darkness, this was light, someone kind and ready to comfort the distress. Emmanuel sat down on a step and embraced the little one, allowing him to sob against his chest. It wasn't Emmanuel who did this. It was the clown, and there was no way that Emmanuel would condone that. It was wrong.

I could see the clown looking up into the stalls. He was laughing, mocking us, as though it was a good trick, that he had outsmarted us. He couldn't have gotten away with doing it to a little girl, but somehow, he got away with doing it to a boy. Like a victorious gladiator, he raised his hands over his head, to demand that the crowd respond, to whip up applause over his disgusting act.

As he did so, Emmanuel stood and silently looked in his direction. The triumphant sweep of his arms was abruptly arrested. The applause, already feeble, died, giving way to a stunned silence. Everybody's attention turned towards the man holding the little one in his arms and the clown faded into insignificance. There was a dignified authority on Emmanuel that demanded respect. It was given without hesitation, the crowd relieved to be excused from responding to the clown's manipulation.

The sudden stillness also caught the little one's attention and he lifted his eyes from the damp shirtfront he had been hiding in to look up into his rescuer's face. It somehow gave him the courage to scan the now silent stands, and then to hazard a glance in the direction of the ring. What he saw was amazing. The clown was retreating! His stage paint, the perpetual leer, was melting, distorting into an unrecognizable mess, revealing the fear and shame on his face. The clown could no longer hide what he really was.

It had only appeared as if he was getting away with it. His private life was a mess, riddled with pain. It was hollow and empty. He had to make people laugh, that was his job, but how he went about doing it wasn't honourable. It was a low act. A good act will receive applause and even long afterwards the memory of it will bring a smile. Not this act. Not everybody in the audience had laughed, not at all. Even the people who did laugh didn't do it for long and there was nothing for them to take away to enjoy again later. This was unquestionably a low, cheap trick.

As I watched the scene, I could feel the anger returning. *Serve him right, he deserves everything he got, and more!* I could feel the twisting in my gut at the thought. I wanted to hurt him, hurt him bad. Vengeful, hateful thoughts of hurting this miserable creature that had damaged me so much roiled through me.

As they did, I became a little boy once again. I wrestled with the thoughts as I sat in the safety of Emmanuel's arms. He didn't say anything, but slowly I became aware of his breath against my cheek and, as I did so, I remembered the dream. The worms, the insects eating me away, this is what they were: my judgements and hatred of the clown!

"It's not doing you any good, you know." His words were gentle, for my ears only, but I knew he was right. This had been keeping me stuck, and it wasn't worth the effort it took to maintain the inner rage. I had been spinning my wheels long enough. I had thought letting go of the anger would let the clown off scot free' but instead it was holding me bound to him, letting his power over me continue. No more! I gave an enormous internal heave to push the blackness away from me and, as I did, Emmanuel backed me up, giving me strength beyond my own to throw off the darkness. Light washed around us, a bright and happy aura spreading, embracing us, clean and refreshing.

"Well done!" Emmanuel's encouragement was just what I needed. I stood once more beside him, the little one still in his arms.

"I'm proud of you, too." I grinned at my counterpart. Somehow it had been a team effort. Together we did it, Emmanuel and me—or us—it didn't seem to matter. Bits of me that I was discovering were getting to know Emmanuel, and we ended up together in the end, anyway.

Emmanuel was looking out over the circus arena, and I followed his gaze. Was there another piece of me stranded out there?

"What do we need to do?" There was a dark cloud still hanging over the arena. I got the uncomfortable feeling we would need to go down there.

"Yes, we need to retrieve what was left behind."

As I peered into the murky cloud, I could make out something lying on the ground. We retraced our steps, moving towards the shadows, facing the darkness together, the little part of me safely in Emmanuel's arms.

The clown retreated from us. I had been a harmless little boy when he had pulled down my pants, but he had not counted on Emmanuel. He had bitten off more than he could chew with this one!

Something of myself had been left behind in my haste to escape the ring, but I was not sure if it was a part of me or a garment of some kind. I squinted into the shadows trying to make it out as we continued towards the clown, who cowered away from us now, and whatever we needed to reclaim. A vague Sunday School memory surfaced of David facing off against Goliath, or maybe when he rescued the lamb from the lion. They had been favourite stories many years ago. They fitted the scene that was unfolding as we purposefully moved in the clown's direction. This had been a giant to me, this sorry piece of humanity, trembling and bleating as he backed away from our advance.

"Now, this is the fun part." I could hear the stern tone in Emmanuel's voice. He was not someone to be messed with and I felt my own courage increasing. I was going back into the place that I had been running from to take back what was mine.

Emmanuel took up his position between me and the clown as I stooped over the abandoned object. It was a cloak, or coat of some kind, not a little person as I had thought. As I touched it, shimmering colours erupted, the full spectrum of the rainbow, dancing in the folds as if they were alive. "It's beautiful, wonderfully beautiful." I could only whisper.

At that the clown fled. His headlong flight was driven by black things that had surrounded him and had driven him to his destructive life. He had wanted that coat. Seeing me with Emmanuel retrieving what was mine was too much for him and he hightailed it out of there.

Emmanuel held out the coat so I could slip my arms into the big sleeves.

"Is this really mine? Did I really leave this behind? I didn't know I had one of these." I stared down at the pulsating colours.

"Yes. This is yours. This is what you left behind."

"It's a bit big." The sleeves extended way past my fingers and the hem draped along the ground like a wedding train.

"You'll grow into it. This is about authority. Do you remember the Commander? He will wear this cloak. This is his authority that was stolen from him. He will continue to grow into it."

The circus ring felt lighter, cleaner, and the coat reflected colours that were glowing with beautiful light to every corner of the big top. They were not the gaudy lights of the grubby side-show, or the flashy showiness of the glitzy circus acts. There was purity in them. Together we turned our back on the spot where the clown had been and made our way towards the steps once more. The little boy made his way towards mum and dad holding Emmanuel's hand, walking, not fleeing this time. Mum had come running down the steps and opened her arms wide to welcome the brave little boy back into her embrace.

I knew he was safe.

CALEB

The same four angels, who had moved the tree, picked the Roller up and put her back on track as if she weighed no more than a matchbox car. It was as easy as that. They wore white gloves, handling her almost reverently. They took up their post at each corner of the car, dusting off their gloves as if to say "Okay, that's done. What's next?"

It felt so good to be back, facing the right way, the open road clear in front of us. A glorious day, extraordinary scenery, and the perfect touring vehicle made an amazing combination. I felt as light as air. What more could you want! And the company wasn't half bad, either.

We got into the luxurious car ready to head off once more.

"Just before we go, let's have a quick look at that dream again." Emmanuel's suggestion didn't seem daunting, and I readily agreed.

This time was very different. I could easily crawl out of the narrow sleeping bag, exposing a mess of insects and worms. Getting the man's attention was no longer difficult, not a bad joke. His wife came out and poured the ointment on, slathered it on like it was shaving cream until I was covered with it halfway up to my knees. I protested that it was expensive stuff, and I didn't want her to waste it, but no, she was determined to be generous, telling me she had plenty. Underneath the ointment my skin became pink and perfect with not a trace of the offensive insects or worms.

"Wow! This is amazing," I grinned at Emmanuel. "I feel so much lighter."

He grinned back. "I'm sure you do. It's always good to get rid of that sort of junk."

"This has got to make a difference." He readily agreed.

Chapter Seventeen

Riding a wave of inspiration when momentum and vision work together to get results is one thing; plodding without it is a whole other. Completing this renovation had nothing of the exhilaration, the vibe of creativity. It was all just hard slog, dogged determination fuelling the decision to move forward every day. Don't get me wrong; we made progress. But it was hard. It was very much the 'building block' thing but I did feel lighter in myself, more able to see a way through.

The engineer came, a funny little man in tight pants and platform shoes like a throwback from the 1970s. Some fashion should be buried forever in my opinion. He minced around with his clipboard, muttering to himself before handing down his verdict. He charged me a lot of money for the privilege of complicating my life. As I had suspected, we needed to do a lot of underpinning. He suggested even more drainage and a whole raft of things to both make allowance for movement and to stop it from happening in the first place. The foundations had never been done properly. Oh, they were completed to the regulations of the day, but they were totally inadequate to handle such reactive clay soil.

Like I said it was hard.

Someone else could have patched it all up, quickly put it on the market, and let the new buyer worry about it, but I couldn't do that. Never could I do that.

Every day felt like I was wading through thick syrupy mud that impeded each forward step.

Half the time I was undoing previously completed work. I was cutting up perfectly good walls to put in new expansion joints; ripping down recently installed cornice to put up shadow line, a sleek modern alternative to cornice that could allow for some movement; repainting—again; and digging up the driveway to make way for more and even deeper drains. The heavy machinery churned up the lawn and decimated garden beds. A bucket load of our hard-earned money was flying out the window in the process. We didn't have some unending supply of money. This felt like madness!

Out of the rubble a home was emerging. Slowly but surely, we were making headway.

The kitchen had finally arrived and had been installed. The dining and family areas were finished. The flooring was down. The main bedroom was great. It was so much better than a mattress on the floor surrounded by mystery boxes. But everything just felt hard! Why was it all so hard?

I was too afraid to really enjoy our achievements. Sarah enthused about them all. She spoke in superlatives. I could only acknowledge them as okay. I felt so vulnerable.

During this whole time, we hadn't been entertaining. It's not so inspiring when you can't even offer a guest a clean place to sit down.

But now? Sarah couldn't wait any longer. She was so thrilled with her new kitchen. It had to be celebrated, in Sarah's opinion anyway. She was so excited;

I was not. I had enough on my plate.

So, out came the list. She is good at lists.

Sarah had created some art and wanted help hanging pictures. She wanted this done and that done.

"Caleb, could you do this?" "Caleb, could you move that?" "Please, Caleb… Caleb… Caleb…

Why did all these things have to be finished just because some of her family members were coming? So many extra projects! For goodness' sake! I did not need this.

Aurora was also coming home for the weekend. It would be so good to see her. The moment she arrived she got busy in the kitchen with her mother.

Soon the house was full. They all wanted the grand tour. Inevitably, they wanted to see everything. It was Sarah's uncle, Andrew, who put into words what I knew they were all thinking.

"Why hasn't he finished yet, huh? Why is it taking so long? I would have thought you would have had it done ages ago." He didn't say it to my face. No, he said it to Sarah—loudly—so I could hear.

I turned on my heel and walked out of the room before I said or did something I would regret. Aurora saw the exchange and followed me.

"It's okay, Dad. He couldn't possibly understand."

"I wish he would just dry up. Miserable old coot."

Family—good food—I love Sarah's family. Sarah had excelled herself. It was a party, but I was in no mood for a party. It did not feel like a good time to me. Like I said, everything was hard, and I couldn't escape it any more than I could escape this little family shindig.

After the last person finally left and the cleaning up was finished, I lay in bed for a long time staring up at the ceiling. I had taken such pride in my previous builds, but this had none of that. Every single time I completed something, I wondered if I would have to pull it apart and redo it.

Thoughts of the bike, my great childhood desire, floated through my dazed over-worked mind.

"Emmanuel, does this have anything to do with how I am feeling? Would you help me please?" I smiled my gratitude into the darkness, knowing that he heard me, that he cared.

~

The familiar feel of the Roller's leather seat and the warmth of Emmanuel's smile greeted me. We talked for a bit, backwards and forwards before I bought up the subject of the bike.

"Did you want to look at it?"

"Yes, I think I do. I've remembered it a few times just lately."

As we spoke, the memory began to replay.

~

"Caleb!" I could hear my mother calling me from her position at the back door as I scurried around the side of the house to avoid detection.

"Caleb!!" She called again as I pushed past the english may bush, and moved towards the place where I had my scooter. I went the long way 'round the house, avoiding the path past the privet bush. It was better to run the gauntlet of the bees erupting from the may bush than get too close to the privet. That wretched shrub was also flowering. Its pungent smell was even more dominant than the pervasive farm smells. Every year it brought on my asthma, every single year. Anything I could do to avoid it was worth the detour.

I heard Mum making her way down the wide veranda towards the side of the house, her footsteps echoing on the timber decking.

"Caleb! Where are you going? *Caleb*! Come here, Caleb!" Mum yelled, scanning the yard for any sign of me. She absentmindedly wiped her hands on her apron as her scowl swept across the large garden. When there was no reply. She gave up, as I knew she would.

"Make sure you're home by five!" The last-minute instruction was thrown over her shoulder as she turned to go.

"Yeah, Mum," I half-heartedly muttered under my breath. The noise was enough to disturb a blue-tongue lizard that hissed at me in disgust. I had caught him off guard, sunbaking in a patch of late spring sunshine.

"You'd better watch out, Mister, or the chook shed cats will find you," I told him. I had seen a big blue-tongue hibernating under the wood heap earlier in the year and I thought this was probably the same one. In the cooler months, I could touch them, but the warm weather was enough to make this big fella more agile and he easily evaded me, disappearing into the shrubbery.

I heard the back screen door slam as Mum retreated inside, her attempt at producing compliance from me abandoned.

I made my way towards my escape machine and glared down balefully at the scooter. It was tired and battered now, its solid wheels had chunks of rubber missing and its red paint was faded and scratched. It had been a birthday present several years earlier and, even then, not what I had wanted. I had asked for a bike! A two-wheeler like my mates had but, no, I got a scooter instead.

It didn't even have pump-up tyres. For years now, I had struggled along the dusty back roads around our property, trailing along behind my friends. Still, it helped get me away from the farm, away from the chooks, and away from that blasted privet.

Friday! Maybe on Friday I will get the bike he promised me. My upcoming birthday had been my chance to raise the subject again. I was turning twelve. It had been on the list almost every birthday and Christmas since I was about six, when I had first been promised one. The bike, always the bike, kept returning to my wish list. When the bike hadn't been forthcoming, I had tried for other things: a pony, a go-cart, anything to get me some sense of freedom. I had been given a go-cart for Christmas a couple of years back, but that had been hard work and knocked me up too quickly. No one wanted to push me around for too long if I couldn't also take a turn at pushing them. It sat under the tree where I had left it, abandoned to the elements. Now I was back harping on about the bike. It had started as soon as I had dumped my school bag near the back door and made my way to the kitchen. The smell of fresh baking wafted towards me. I launched into my speech as I reached for a handful of freshly baked Anzac biscuits.

"Please, Mum, can I have a bike for my birthday? Please? Everyone else has got one. Please, Mum?" I stuffed a biscuit into my mouth as I talked. I had long since given up asking Dad, choosing to sweet talk Mum instead.

"Mum, Dad promised. Please?"

"Hello, Caleb. How was your day?"

"Aw, Mum."

"Caleb!"

"Mum, I just want a bike! Please, Mum!" I couldn't keep the whine from my voice.

"That's enough biscuits, son."

"Mum, please?"

"We'll see."

I don't know how many times we had repeated the conversation. I was getting desperate. I was almost in high school, and I didn't have my own wheels yet. I had already been driving an old, abandoned car around the deserted dirt tracks and I still had no pushbike!

Mum turned her attention back to her baking as I stuffed some more biscuits in my pocket and made my escape.

Now, as I pulled out the old scooter and made my way towards the road, I racked my brain for anything else I could do. I just had to get that bike! The scooter may not have been much, embarrassingly so, but it was all I had. I just had to get away. I knew my way around; I knew which places to avoid: the neighbour's photinia hedge, the black wattle that bloomed in winter, the

Jasmine cascading over a fence near my school. Mostly, it was the chook sheds and the farm I shunned. The dust that the chickens produced pervaded the whole farm, but the dander was unbearable in the sheds.

I had nagged about the privet bush too, asking dad to cut it down, asking mum to ask dad. It never worked. The privet bush remained to taunt me year after year.

I spent the afternoon at my mate Anthony's place, mucking around with his slingshot, laughing ourselves silly watching 'The Three Stooges on telly, devouring his mum's biscuits, and riding his brother's bike as I dreamed of owning my own. It wasn't until his mum called him inside to have dinner that I realized it was past 5 o'clock.

When I got home the rest of the family had already eaten and my father had returned to the shed to finish packing the last of the eggs. I endured the predictable lecture from Mum as I ate my dinner and decided not to raise the subject of the bike again until after the dust had settled. It was much better to wait until she wasn't annoyed with me.

I had no sooner downed the last of my lamb chop and vegies than it came.

"Caleb, would you go and help your dad in the shed, please?"

The packing shed wasn't any better than the chook sheds. The resident cat family helped keep the mice and rats under control. Cat dander and the dust that had accumulated over years made it a very unpleasant place to be. Even the cats were unpleasant, skulking around the edges, giving a demanding yowl every now and then. The wild-eyed felines tolerated humans warily, hanging around waiting to be fed the broken eggs thrown in their direction. They were certainly not sweet, domesticated moggies.

"Aw Mum! Do I have to?" I whined.

"Yes, go on son. He's been out there all day and he could do with some help."

I didn't move from my place at the table, picking up a comic book and distracting myself.

CALEB

This scenario had been repeated so many times. A few years ago, it had been a ritual at least once a day, trying to get me into the chook sheds to help Dad. I would reluctantly make a start only to begin wheezing almost immediately. The dust and the smells of the chooks were a killer combination. They worked every time, conspiring to bring on the dreaded asthma. I wasn't asked as often now. Mum knew…

So, we played the game: her dutifully asking, and me evading. I did it well, I did it often and I did it at every opportunity. When Dad's brother, Uncle Harry, visited he was even worse than Mum. He never missed a chance to tell me off for not helping my dad. "You should…" "Why don't you ever…?" "In my day…" "You lazy boy, go and help in the sheds…" "Go and help your dad." "You should… You should…"

Dad never said anything; he didn't ask me himself, but I knew Mum spoke for him.

"Caleb." I had begun to move towards the living room when mum spotted me. My ploy had not gone unnoticed. I made some sort of noise indicating assent and waited until my mother was distracted with my baby brother, born many years after my sister and me. As with most things my mother asked of me, if I ignored them for long enough, I could get away with it, mostly.

Sometimes it was unavoidable, and I would end up in the shed working with Dad. Well, not exactly with him. There seemed to be no good reason to be there, putting elastic bands on egg cartons or something dumb like that. I would, maybe, pack a few eggs. I was meant to be helping but I did not feel welcome. He continued with his tasks, his old-fashioned music playing on the ancient radio, his head down and absorbed in his work. He never said very much and just expected me to do the same, I guess. I never lasted for long before my wheezing drove me back into the house. *Did dad think I was pretending so I could get out of helping; that I was somehow bringing on the asthma?* I never found out.

Just a few days away from my twelfth birthday and I had already become an expert at avoiding, evading, ducking, and weaving my way out of responsibility, out of discipline, and out of painful situations. I thought I was pretty clever, really; that I was good at outsmarting people, particularly authority figures.

I kept badgering Mum about the bike, and she kept prevaricating. As my birthday approached, the tension inside of me mounted. I had done a scan around the farm, wondering if I might see evidence of that longed-for gift. No go! Either it was so well hidden I couldn't find it, or dad hadn't… and Mum wasn't giving anything away.

I can't stand it! The desperation had increased with each day, until now I was at breaking point. It was all I could think about, day and night. Another disappointment. *No*!!! I felt like I would break in two if I didn't get that bike!

Another broken promise; another setback; another blow; "I can't! *I can't do it*!!!"

The night before my birthday I collared Mum again. I started out okay, asking, well harassing really, like I had been each day, but when she, again, evaded my question I came unglued.

"Mum, please tell me he bought me a bike! Please Mum!" By this time, I was crying.

"Mum, please? He promised me." She held me as I wept, sobbing against her as I hadn't done since I was little.

The bicycle, when it finally arrived the next day, was almost an anticlimax. The fear of another disappointment had been so acute that it had stolen much of the joy. Although it was second-hand when I got it, repainted, and fixed up, and without the gears I had hoped for, I sure put a lot more miles on that thing. It finally gave me some sense of freedom, an escape from the farm.

Something from much earlier invaded the memory. I was twirling around, free-falling backwards. As I watched, I could taste the terror.

CALEB

I saw a baby fighting, with arms and legs flailing. A tiny one in the womb, struggling, but it didn't last for long. Soon there was no fight left. The battle, the fight to live, had continued for too long. As I watched, it diminished, and the struggling became fitful and weak.

The baby had become tangled up with the cord, like a dolphin caught in a net. I watched—horrified. There were no words—the emotions—the nothingness— was overwhelming.

Emmanuel's presence enveloped me, and I knew he would help me, just like he said he would.

The emotions the baby and I were feeling were cataclysmic. He needed me— the adult-me— to find words for it; I needed to give the little one a voice.

"Who am I?"

"Not safe…"

"Nobody wants me."

"I don't belong."

"Abandoned…"

Each thought came slowly to the surface, wrestled from the depths of my being. The emotional place, like the epicentre of an earthquake, was shaking me to the core with its intensity.

I could only stay briefly before turning away, looking into Emmanuel's eyes, drawing strength, resting a moment, then returning to the little one.

"Disconnected…"

"That's it! I'm not connected."

Repeatedly I escaped back to the safety of Emmanuel before returning to the fray.

"I don't know if there will be anyone there to catch me."

"Is there anyone who cares?"

"Dad. Are you there?"

"Dad."

Nothing. No response.

"Does anybody want me?"

The earthquake intensified. Fissures extended their reach, exposing the fractured, damaged foundations of my life, the very core of my being.

"Help me." Adult-me voiced the unspoken cry of the unborn baby.

Emmanuel's response was immediate. He began unravelling the cord, very gently, first around my hand, then my neck… He sat me up a little bit and pulled it off my chest. Slowly, gradually, his touch light and his hands cool against my agitated body.

He didn't cut it. He unravelled the umbilical cord. It was a life source baby-me still needed. I lay across his knee, limp and inert, while he worked. He was there, very present, his gentle words soothing, comforting, and bringing life. He lifted me and laid my tiny body against his chest and covered me with his hands, skin on skin. The gentle crooning continued, blended with his heartbeat.

As I watched the constriction being lifted from the baby's chest and neck, I found myself taking deep breaths as if for the first time.

I knew he would stay there for as long as it took for me to recuperate, and it would take some time. This was not a quick fix. This was a complete reconstruction. Again, it was at the very foundation of my life.

"I will never be far away. I'm not going to leave you." His voice and his touch soothed me. My frantic heartbeat gradually calmed. This was very deliberate, hands-on, and intensive.

I could leave this part of me with Emmanuel. I knew he was safe.

Understanding began to flow into my thoughts as I continued to experience the harrowing emotions.

My whole life had been a search, a quest to know. So many questions.

Who am I? Where do I belong? Is there anybody who wants me?

CALEB

I guess I had some sort of connection when I was inside mum but with mum's fear, high blood pressure and sugar hits, even the womb felt completely unsafe, even deadly. That was the reason I was thrashing around so much. But outside was terrifying. I didn't want to be born.

It was best described as a vacuum, a black hole of nothingness. *I am not in a vacuum. I am the vacuum.* That has been my quest: to somehow fill that void, to prove that I deserved to exist, that I belonged.

Who am I? I had always been looking for something to make a statement, and then support the story. I wanted to be heard; I wanted to be listened to.

When my needs were not met, the walls came up, deep, fortified, and impenetrable. *If you reject me, I will reject you.*

There had been an urgent need to be better than others, always trying to be better than others. To get things *right*! Then I would be somebody, I would be okay. Where I couldn't make the grade, which was often, the asthma helped me. *I can't because…It's not my fault.* I was amazed at how vital that was. It was as if my life depended on it.

Underneath it had all been my fault in some nebulous, inexplicable way. My fault…

This also related to the feelings I woke up with sometimes in the middle of the night. They leaked from the carefully constructed constraints I had built for them.

I would recount missed opportunities and tell myself that if I had done this or that, then I wouldn't be in this situation. I beat myself up. Every failure rubbed my nose in the deep shame of not belonging, of not being wanted.

I had no clue how to reach out past my own blockade to connect with my girls. I tried. I wanted to but—I didn't do it for my girls like my father didn't do it for me.

My Dad was a stranger. He left me to my own devices, and Mum gave up. She tried, but I think I blocked her out. She nagged a lot but didn't follow through. I know I didn't make her life easy.

"Emmanuel! I can't do this! I can't!" The angst that I felt was fresh, raw and exposed. My emotions spilled out as I returned to the Roller.

"That's true. You can't." He didn't seem at all fazed by my blubbering. He held me as I sobbed, as my mother had done. I hadn't cried like this, from the depths of me, deep shoulder-shaking sobs, for a long time.

"The way I was raised hasn't helped me," I said, when I finally caught my breath.

"I don't blame them particularly. I was a brat of a kid. Mum told me a while ago she never knew what to do with me. The asthma sure didn't help any. I get why Dad just hid in the shed." I was catching a glimpse of how my parents may have felt.

"But I don't know what to do! I'm still not getting it! Sometimes it feels like God has a big stick and…" I hit my knee with my hand, as if I was swatting a fly.

"He doesn't have to do that. Sin has its own punishment."

"What do you mean? I don't get it."

"Discipline is your friend." He had made this statement before. I hadn't understood it then, and I didn't understand it now.

"It's not a legalistic thing, just a set of rules and regulations. There is life in it," he continued. "It takes a lot of love and commitment to train a child and my Papa is a good dad. You can't separate discipline from love. Discipline without love is abusive and 'love' without discipline isn't love either. You have thought of discipline as being punishment, but it is not the same thing. My Dad has a lot of authority He wants to give you, but He can't do that unless you learn this."

"I did okay when I was in business. How come it's not working now?" I asked.

CALEB

"You had a framework that you worked in, and it worked for you. Now the discipline has to come from the inside, not from the outside. That's where it wasn't built when you were a kid. That's what we are working on now, to build the internal framework."

"I feel like I have been twisted out of shape and that there is no fixing it. Like a tree that has grown around an obstacle. I've grown up crooked! I am warped. How do you relearn something as basic as this when I didn't learn it as a kid? This is not hard. It's *impossible*!" I exploded in exasperation.

"Yes, you're right. Isn't it great?"

"*What*?" I stared at the man, completely unsettled by his statement.

"Do you remember the little blue bottle I gave you?"

"Umm" I racked my brain trying to think where I had put it. I had stuffed it in my pocket and hadn't given it another thought. I rummaged around first in one, and then another of the roomy pockets in my jacket. Finally, I pulled it out. It was exquisite and, absentmindedly, I admired the beauty of the workmanship.

"You're meant to use it."

"How?"

"You pour it over yourself."

"But? What is it? How does it work?" I stared at the sapphire blue liquid in the tiny bottle.

"God knew you couldn't do it. He knew you wouldn't be able to get it so He made it possible."

"So, what is it?" I asked again.

"It's called grace and there is an unlimited supply to help you whenever you need it."

"It seems like I need it all the time."

"Yep! You've got it. That's it; all the time. Grace makes it all possible."

"How does it work?"

"Grace is wonderfully upside-down to what you are used to. First, you let

God give to you and then you can do, not the other way around. First, you receive. It's not about trying to make yourself do what you feel you should, the rules you try to impose on yourself, or others try to impose on you. The rules and regulations don't work; they never have. The new framework on the inside grows out of relationship, out of receiving. Grace is what gives you the desire, the willingness, the capacity, the strength, and the determination to see it through. You will never be able to really trust without this."

I looked at him, trying to absorb what he was saying. I knew I would need to digest this conversation for some time.

Miraculously, Emmanuel had helped me get past my own defences and survival strategies. He knew me even when I didn't know myself. He had caught me in my free-fall into nothingness, into the abyss. He had helped me. Somehow, I knew I was going to be okay.

CALEB

Chapter Eighteen

So now everything was going to be just wonderful, right? You know, happily ever after? Ummm, maybe not quite.

They were better though. I had more resilience and a little bit more humanity. Sarah noticed a difference.

Still, it takes time and effort to change the well-worn paths of negative thinking and lies, and the journey was an ongoing one.

Grace, the upside-down concept Emmanuel had spoken of, was something I knew was important. Some days I remembered, but on others I forgot.

I decided to put aside trading for a time and focus on the outside of the house. The renovation of the inside was complete. Now the orange-toned roof was repointed, and painted a pleasing grey, and the exterior was bagged and painted. I inserted panels of board in several places that gave a bit of architectural contrast but also allowed for movement. It looked great, and so very different to the orange-toned house that had made such a glaring statement in the landscape. After a few months, I could count on my fingers the bigger jobs left to be done.

We now turned our attention to completing the garden. I created wide steps leading up to the side of the house. Several trees had not survived the drought and were removed. Together we weeded, pruned, and planted.

One weekend, we had been working well together for most of the day when it happened. I just expected Sarah to work like one of the blokes. You know, understand what to do next without any instruction. I needed her to direct me as I reversed my very full trailer. I didn't hit anything, but she made a job that should have been easy into something difficult. She didn't seem to get 'left hand down', 'right hand down', and she kept disappearing out of view of my mirrors. It was so frustrating! I was a bit harsh with her when she got it wrong for about the third time. It wasn't the only thing that happened that day either.

Sarah was upset that night, really upset. She wasn't throwing accusations at me like she used to do. She just quietly sobbed and talked about her longing for more. I'm just not the romantic type, or even very sensitive, come to that. I missed out on that when it was being handed out, I guess.

"I need you to be kind to me. I can't know what your grunts mean! You have to tell me what you expect me to do. I don't know by osmosis! And I need encouragement, not just you telling me what I've done wrong! It feels like you only see what mistakes I make and not what I do well." She blew her nose loudly. "I feel like we have had this same conversation so many times. I respond to gentleness. You melt my heart when you are gentle to me, but when you speak to me that way, I just wither inside."

I listened woodenly as she spoke, not knowing how to respond.

"I need you to give me a hug—please." She was cutting me some slack.

I reached for her, still feeling like a lump of wood. She leaned her face into my shoulder, smearing tears and mascara on my shirt.

"I'm sorry…" I trailed off. It wasn't much of an apology, but it was the best I could do.

After a while, I could feel the tension begin to ease from her body as I held her. She was right. We had had this conversation many times.

I put Sarah off, I protect myself from her. Her expectations of me were a huge distraction from where I was going, what I was doing. If I got hooked into what Sarah wanted there would be something else and then, something else. *Either I do what she wants, or I do what I want. It is either-or. And it feels like, if I start on that track, the requirements will never stop. Ever! The list will just keep growing. But I also expect her to know what I want and know what to do.*

Yep… We have had this conversation before a time or two—or three. I remember for a bit, maybe, and I try for a while, but…

I stayed up for a while after Sarah went to bed and I decided to ask Emmanuel about it.

"I don't know how to love her!" I was exasperated when I spoke to him, sitting beside me in the Roller. "I get so angry with her sometimes."

"True."

"She stuffed it up! I could have taken out the corner of those steps! I only just finished them."

"Did you give her any instruction?"

"No. She shouldn't need me to hold her hand!"

"Why do you need to blame her then?" I couldn't answer that one.

We were pulled up in the middle of the road. Not that there was any choice. The road, if you could call it that, was incredibly narrow with nowhere to pull over. Up ahead there was a corner and not just any corner. The track was already slippery and treacherous but this corner, it was a doozy. A land slip had loosened a large rock, and it sat like a sentinel against the steep wall right on the hairpin bend where it had fallen. Precarious, loose debris looked

CALEB

ready to hurtle down the slope at any provocation. A stream of water, diverted by the stubborn rock, ran perpetually from the mountain, and had severely eroded the track. There was no guard rail, of course, and the near side edge looked very soft and fell away into thin air. If you were looking for a place to park or to take in the spectacular view, this was not it.

I stared at the hairpin bend ahead of us on the track. I felt completely intimidated by it.

"It isn't as hard as it seems." Yet again, he answered my thoughts.

"Is there another way?"

"Sure. You can go backwards."

"What is that supposed to mean?" I could feel my hackles coming up.

"Anger leads to hatred and its ultimate end is murder. The whole thing is fuelled by blame-shifting. It's a broad road, so there are plenty that go that way. This road is very narrow because so few bother to find it. If you make the choice to navigate it, you will make it a bit wider and easier for others to follow. Loving your wife does not come naturally, not to anyone, and you were never shown how. I can help you."

"Murder!" I had got completely stuck on that word. "You must be kidding me!"

I snapped out of the vision. I wasn't ready to look at that little number just now. All the next week I found myself seething, snapping, testy. I knew it. Sarah knew it. Anyone who encountered me knew it. It wasn't like I was ready to kill anyone, but my attitude was certainly destructive. There was enough seismic activity to send shock waves in all directions. I seemed to trigger Sarah at every turn. I was single-handedly demolishing the relationship that had begun to blossom between us. Not that I could see that. I was too busy blaming everyone else.

She kindly pointed it out to me in slow, single syllables, easy to understand

and at a volume that could be heard about a mile away.

I thought maybe, just maybe, she was right. I needed to finish my little chat with Emmanuel and have another look at that despicable corner.

We were still sitting smack bang in the middle of the track right where I had left it. Emmanuel seemed genuinely pleased to see me. Why on earth would he want to see me when I was being such a #%&#?

"Do you remember the cricket bat?"

"Oh, yes." It was not one of my better moments.

Christmas school holidays were the best! Yahoo! No more teachers, no more books for weeks! But first, there was Christmas. It was worth enduring the scrub up, the uncomfortable clothes, and the inevitable family visitors. Christmas meant the best feed of the year and presents, something new to play with.

The year I got a new cricket set, I was maybe 10 or so. It was a beauty. It was full size with lots of spring. It may have even been English willow. I was so proud of it. I had been given something that I actually wanted, something valuable. It gave me value too, somehow.

I couldn't wait to show my mates. I could just imagine them admiring it. The only trouble was, they were away for the holidays. Anthony had headed to Terrigal with his family and Trevor was in the Blue Mountains somewhere. The chooks weren't going anywhere so we weren't either—ever. No, that's not true. We went to Canberra and the Snowy Mountains for a holiday one time. It was a disaster.

Every year, we had some group of cousins or other come to visit for the holidays. Both my parents came from large families so there were plenty to go around. If we ran out of cousins, there were people who knew Dad who would bring their kids. It was torture. As the farm was close to the beach, I'm sure it was a great arrangement, but I hated it. They were almost inevitably girls! I was meant to entertain them! Mostly, they were my sister's age, a couple of years younger than me, and they were clueless when it came to cricket. Or they were older, and they thought they knew better. I resented the whole arrangement. It was so frustrating, and they would not do it right.

Pam was one of the older girls. She wasn't one of the cousins, just some other random girl. She ruined my cricket bat! She used the back of it to whack the stumps back in! That is not what you do! She left my beautiful, brand new cricket bat with heaps of dings in it. There were indentations all over it!

I was furious. My bellowing rant bought the game to an abrupt end. I badly wanted her to pay.

"You stupid girl! You idiot! What do you think you're doing?" The girls scattered before my assault, like leaves in the wind, running snivelling to their mummies. The girls had not a single good thing to say about me. I didn't care. I didn't want them there in the first place.

There was no one for me to go to. What would have been the point of that anyway? There was no one to help bring any sense of perspective. It was all raw emotion. Going to dad didn't even enter my head. Mum was busy with visitors.

So I went to the dog. I buried my tear-stained face into her long fur, and quietly stoked the fire under the cauldron of my resentment and rage. The patient border collie whined softly and turned to lick the tears streaming from my face. Tessie loved me, she seemed to understand, but she couldn't help me comprehend the choices I was making. An ugly brew was churning inside me, colouring my view of women and girls.

I came back to the Roller, but I did not want to look at Emmanuel. He sat there, as patiently as Tessie had. As the anger roiled in me, thoughts of long-ago girlfriends who had dumped me, and betrayed me, came flooding back, incidents with Sarah and the girls.

The venom came spewing out in putrid waves. The words tumbled over themselves heavy with judgement, accusations, and blame. I had fermented quite a concoction. Emmanuel absorbed them like Tessie's fur had absorbed my tears.

"Why can't I ever have something good just for me? Why does someone have to come and spoil it for me?" Releasing the fetid tide of words finally caused the intensity of the anger to ebb. My sense of equilibrium was beginning to return when the thought of forgiving them crossed my consciousness. Anger erupted again at the unwelcome thought.

"If I let go of this, they will get off scot free. It's no skin off their nose. I just get lumped with it." I ranted.

"The girls lost out too, you know."

"How?" I swung around to glare at him, but his eyes caught me. They were so full of compassion. My bluster began to fall away. Finally, I was ready to listen. My perspective needed some shifting.

"You are trading in the wrong currency." His comment came out of left field.

"What? What do you mean?"

"You and Sarah both use different currency to trade with. It's about what you both value."

"I don't get it." I stared at him, nonplussed.

"Do you remember the coins you found and how you tried to buy lollies with them?"

"Yes. They were Spanish coins if I remember correctly. I didn't get very far with those little tarnished discs. The old guy in the shop had quite a time trying to convince me that I couldn't buy anything," I mused.

Emmanuel laughed softly. "You could take a wheelbarrow load of those things to the corner store and still not be able to buy any sweets, at least not in Australia."

"So, what do I need to do?"

"Come to me and we can trade."

For some reason I felt I would have nothing of value to trade with. Like the couple of foreign coins I had held so tightly in my grubby little hand, everything I had seemed worthless: I was bankrupt.

I think he is talking heavenly again. I have nothing.

"How?"

"I have paid the full price. You can come anytime, and buy with no money, everything you need."

He turned his hands over as he spoke. There were gaping wounds in each hand, still fresh with blood, large enough to fit my index finger. All I could do was stare. I gagged, transfixed by the horror.

How had I not seen them before? Who did this to him? Why?

"It happened because people are incredibly important to me, to both my Dad and I." He answered my thoughts.

I tore my eyes away from the gory sight to look into his face.

"Caleb, people will always have more value than things."

His words penetrated me. "That's what Sarah thinks too," I realized. "That's her currency."

We talked for a long time backwards and forwards, about Sarah, my mum, about Pam and others. My viewpoint, so deeply imbedded, was shifting. Finally, I was able to let go of my judgment and anger.

I made a decision. I would rather be on the right track and fail at it than be on the wrong one and continue as before. The angry road that ended in murder would do untold damage long before it took a life. I didn't want that.

The afternoon was casting its shadows when we got out of the Roller to inspect the hairpin bend more closely. It no longer felt so incredibly daunting. Yes, I needed to take it carefully, to calculate my approach, but it no longer seemed impossible.

We got back into the car, and I slipped her into gear. I looked up. The corner! Where did the corner go? It wasn't there anymore.

"Have a look behind you." I craned my neck around. Sure enough, the hairpin bend I had been dreading was miraculously behind us. The road ahead was clear. I could see more corners ahead, but all were much gentler than the hairpin. Just now, there was a lovely straight to enjoy.

"How did that happen?"

"It's something about making a decision." He winked at me. "Well done."

I just shook my head.

There was even time to savour the Roller and admire the magnificent vista.

"Caleb, you need to take a holiday," he said, out of the blue. As soon as he said it, I knew he was right. A break from the house and its pressures would help both Sarah and me.

Sarah just gave me a knowing look when I told her about what had happened with Emmanuel. She was not at all surprised. She kissed me and accepted my apology without question.

I still had a lot to learn. Both Sarah and I did, but this was such a big step forward. It wasn't the last time I needed to have a little chat with Emmanuel about my relationship with Sarah, but I had made my choice. I wanted to learn.

CALEB

Chapter Nineteen

A family wedding in Queensland provided the perfect excuse to extend the visit into a holiday. Sarah's brother, Jason, and his wife, Anna, had invited us to stay with them. Their beautiful home and their gracious hospitality created the perfect oasis for us. We always felt completely at home with them.

It was a modern, architect-designed home situated in the Gold Coast hinterland with sweeping views towards Morton Bay. The fact that Jason was the builder and his son the architect only added to the experience. Yes, this was exactly what we both needed.

I sat on their deck enjoying an early morning coffee. I started feeling the kinks unwinding, the built-up tension in my shoulders beginning to ease. An eagle's soaring acrobatics caught my attention. It was revelling in the thermals, riding them effortlessly. He made it look so very easy. I knew it wasn't always so. Many years before, I had watched two wedge-tailed eagles on a roadkill. The massive wings heaved in enormous effort to, once again, become airborne. It was cumbersome and ungainly, as different to this easy grace as one could ever imagine. It was as if they didn't belong on the putrid roadkill, earthbound and scavenging. The mammoth exertion had only lifted them as far as some nearby fence posts where they sat and watched as we passed, unwilling to abandon the rotting carcass. Gracefully riding the invisible updrafts, that was their natural element. It was what they were born for.

We returned home after a month feeling rested and revived, ready to tackle the handful of remaining tasks before we could say that the house was completed.

We drove the last few kilometres in driving rain. In the time that we were away, the rains had finally come, breaking the back of the 10-year drought. The sun broke through, low on the horizon, just as we drove into our little town. The creek that our house overlooked had swollen to a gushing, brown and angry torrent. There was no risk of it flooding our home, but we knew others were not so fortunate.

I felt a certain trepidation as I made my way up the broad steps towards the house. If there was ever a test for the foundations, this was it.

Nervously I stepped inside. It was already late, and the light was fading. It took a moment to identify the white debris that was lying on the floor. I flicked on the light switch. My heart sank. This was the nightmare I had dreaded. Chunks of plaster had given way from the newly completed shadow line. There were even traces of pink ceiling insulation in the mess. My attempts at making allowance for movement had been hopelessly inadequate. I willed my eyes to scan the room. Cracks ran haphazard tracks down the corner of the room. They ran their course from the ceiling as if attempting to split the house in two.

Slowly I continued my inspection of the house. Wordlessly Sarah cleaned up the floor. I had been dealt the belly blow that I had feared, and it left me feeling like a child's toy that the family dog had decimated. This could not so easily be swept up and fixed.

"Caleb, would you like something to eat?" I could hear the concern in her voice. I shook my head, unable to face the thought of food.

"Honey, you need to stop now. It's getting late. You'll be able to see much better in the daylight."

I ignored her and continued my obsessive search around the outside of the house by torchlight. Finally, I conceded that she was right. I needed better light. I went to bed, but there was no respite. Sleep refused to come. As the long hours of darkness dragged past, inertia and numbness seeped into my bones, my brain, and my heart.

The morning light confirmed my fears. The clay subsoil had rejected the bounds I had set for it, flexing its strong back upwards at the point where the two roof structures met to form the L shape of the building. The mindless clay had won, empowered by the force of water. Thoroughly defeated, I ceded the fight. I could no longer face another round of repairs. My stomach churned at the thought of it.

What's the point? Everything felt like a complete waste of time. I felt stuck in limbo, a trap of somebody else's creation. Disappointment and discouragement bore down on me, making my limbs heavy and my mind dull. It felt like I had been kicked in the guts and left with my stuffing hanging out.

It took some time before I could go to Emmanuel. I talked to him often, but I couldn't connect in the Roller as I had before. I had dumbed myself down, shut down so completely. I couldn't shut down one part of me without sucking all of me into the quagmire.

I have no idea what I did in that time, just went through the motions, I guess.

∽

When I finally did go to the Roller, he was waiting for me. He didn't say anything, just sat with me. I stared sightlessly

ahead without registering anything for a long time.

A little blue wren caught my eye as he flitted down and sat on the long car bonnet. He darted about with his showy chest flashing brightly in the sun. I couldn't help but be drawn to him. They are such happy little birds. One of his harem joined him, hopping here and there. The little male darted down towards the road at the front of the car. My attention was drawn and finally it registered where we were. There was a broad field in front of us, the largest flat area we had encountered for some time. It may have been a sports field or a camping area. There were people on the far side of the field involved in some sort of activity. The grassed area was mown and well cared for. Directly in front of us was a small creek with steep sides and slippery-looking approaches, more like a ditch than a creek.

"I can't face another obstacle. It's just too hard. It's all we have done. It's been one problem after another." I let out a ragged breath. The pain of the newest cracks was too raw, too close to the surface.

"Would you like to tell me about it?"

I hesitated. He allowed the silence to hang between us. He didn't prompt me. He didn't demand anything. He just waited quietly, with me.

"Maybe I would have been better off demolishing the house and starting again, instead of…" Long, painful pauses punctuated my scattered thoughts and words.

"Maybe I still need to bulldoze it and start again. The money is another thing. Trying to fix the mess has just been good money chasing bad. I don't know what to do."

We sat there for a long time, the two of us. He didn't say much but he was there.

My dad had never been there. Not ever that I could remember, not in good times or in bad.

"I think I want to go now."

"Why don't you do that? I'm here anytime."

"Thank you." I meant it.

~

I'm glad Sarah understood. She didn't put pressure on me. I don't think I could have handled it. I was feeling remarkably flat. I was grateful that the house was habitable, even pleasant to be in except for the cracks, those infernal cracks that gnawed at me daily. I couldn't ignore them. Sarah went about her life, picking up intermittent shifts at work, or gardening and baking. She seemed far less perturbed about the house than I was. Her concern was for me.

"Would now be a good time to tackle the camper trailer you have been talking about? It might give you something to think about other than the house. What do you think?" she suggested one evening.

I didn't give much of a reply, but the thought stuck. I had talked about it previously. We both loved camping and maybe it would give my heart a reason to keep beating.

I spent more time in the Roller with Emmanuel. It wasn't a time for looking at memories or exploring the depths of my heart. It was just a time to be. That was enough. The spiffy little blue wren even came back, showing off in front of us. A small sliver of hope was beginning to grow. Eventually I was ready to move forward. Not with the house, no, but with life. Yes, it was enough.

"Would you like to tackle the creek?" Emmanuel asked casually. He seemed to know that I was ready.

"Yeh, I think I would." There was a lot more room on the other side of the ditch. We walked around the vehicle. The space beside the car was narrow and overgrown. The crossing was too deep to drive straight across. The banks on either side looked slippery with mud. I may have considered it in my big 4x4 if I was in convoy and had the right equipment but…

The other people on the oval; how did they get there, I wonder? I didn't much feel like company just now, not with complete strangers anyway. The cleared area was pretty big. It should be big enough to avoid them. *How do we get across?*

Emmanuel had always managed to work it out before.

"How?"

"Do you reckon I can do it?" There was just a touch of cheekiness in his question.

"Yes. I reckon you can." I gave a short laugh. "You certainly can. I just don't have any idea how."

I turned back towards the Roller. Looking back at me was the grinning face of my old friend the angel. Gee, he was big! His three mates were also there.

I don't know what I expected, but it was not this! We got back in the car and we watched as they threaded two sturdy saplings through the wooden spokes of the wheels. I was incredulous.

Most of the old Rollers I have seen have had metal spokes, but these were timber. It must have been a hardy species of wood to cop all we had given them.

They lifted her effortlessly up onto their shoulders and bore us across the creek like an ancient Egyptian or Roman VIP.

For some reason it tickled me, and I started to laugh. I mean a good, proper laugh. The angels joined us, Emmanuel, and me.

"I think I needed that; thank you guys." They waved and vanished from view as quickly as they had appeared.

"So where to now?" I asked Emmanuel as I surveyed the large grassy area we had crossed to. I still hadn't worked out what sort of place it was. It was well maintained with short inviting lawn. It seemed a friendly sort of place.

"Don't be in any hurry to leave here just yet. There are some things for you here. Give yourself time to just be."

"That sounds good." I responded. Yes, this was a good place to recover a bit. There could even be rainbow trout in the fast-flowing stream I could see on the far side of the field.

"I've been thinking of building a camper trailer. What do you think?" I hesitated before asking the question that I had been mulling over for some time.

"That's a great idea. Go for it. You would enjoy doing that." His encouragement meant a lot.

Together Sarah and I began planning and designing a camper trailer. It took a little while to get the juices flowing again but this was just what the doctor ordered. I love a good project. Helping a friend out in his handyman business also kept a bit of money coming in.

I bought a box-shaped service body that had been used by a telecommunications company on one of their vehicles and it became the base for my fit out. I built a chassis with off-road capability to put the service body on and bolted a rooftop tent on top.

The stainless-steel kitchen was fantastic even in my own estimation. It had a slide-out drawer with a three-burner gas stove, lots of storage space and two good sized fridges. I also had two stainless steel tanks built. I needed help to put together the solar system, and also with the stainless welding, but everything else I could do myself. The whole thing was therapeutic, the designing, the hands-on work, even sourcing equipment like pumps and components.

Every single detail came together so very well. I could look back at the end of each day's work satisfied with the results. It felt good. There was only one small problem. When I tested the stainless tanks, one of them leaked slightly. Darn. It meant returning it to Danny, the man who had done the stainless welding, to be repaired.

Chapter Twenty

On my back. Why? Why am I on my back?

I stared dumbly up at the vast ceiling, blinking away dust that was floating down and settling on my face.

Where am I? Why am I lying down?

My mind groped in slow motion, numbly attempting to grasp what had happened.

Awareness came slowly—the tank—welding—Danny. EXPLOSION!

Disaster had struck. Somehow the tank had exploded. Massively!

I'm not dead, I don't think. I'm still breathing, that's good. Every thought was in slow motion. Severely winded, I hadn't been entirely sure…

Don't move!

Mentally I checked my body.

My head, my eyes, seemed okay. *My right hand—something is wrong. My belly—definitely.*

I wriggled my toes. My legs seemed okay. My ears were ringing like a demented bell tower.

Faintly, as if far away, I could hear voices yelling, footsteps running towards us.

Danny! Is he okay? was my next thought. He had been on the other side of the tank welding!

Gingerly I tried to move, slowly, very slowly pulling myself up to a sitting position.

"Where's my helmet? What happened?" Danny's voice, befuddled and vague, indicated he was still alive.

The stainless tank had been mounted on wooden supports. I had been standing on the other side, watching, while Danny welded the seam that needed repairing. He started at one end, working towards the centre, then began at the other end doing the same. He had just finished, and I remember the red glow beginning to fade, when—BOOM!!

It was not until sometime later that I pieced the story of the unfolding drama together.

The force of the percussion had ripped through the enormous open roller doors, knocking people off their chairs, and equipment to the ground in neighbouring workshops. The wooden supports the tank had been resting on splintered into oblivion, leaving the tank opened up like a tin can. The impact had blown my welding helmet into three pieces, catapulting them in different directions, to the far reaches of the workshop.

The shockwaves resounded through the concrete floor, severe enough to register on seismic detection equipment several kilometres away. Emergency personnel scrambled into action at the news of an explosion. Workmen came running from every direction. Danny's wife, Kaye, told me later she thought several factories, including the large one over the road had pretty much emptied out. I was not even aware of the crowd. Kaye kept the confusion of the brave, the helpful, and the stickybeaks at bay, at the entrance to the big roller door.

A woman from a neighbouring business coolly took control. She assessed our injuries, and then slowly helped us into chairs. Her calm, soothing demeanour helped settle us both. My right hand and wrist had copped the blow and were obviously injured. My thumb stuck out at an odd angle. The full force had been cushioned by my belly which, I have to admit, is somewhat softer than in my younger days. The beginning of an enormous bruise was blooming on my middle.

Danny's injuries, amazingly, were much less. He had bits of shrapnel from his welding helmet imbedded in his forehead, one piece narrowly missing his eye, but that was all. We had no burns, no other physical injuries.

It was not long before I was loaded into an ambulance, one of several that arrived on scene, along with police and fire trucks. The inevitable Occupational Health and Safety Inspector came after the dust had settled and the crowds dispersed. He said that in all his years, he had never been to an explosion as large as that before, where there had not been fatalities. He spent a long time searching the ceiling for signs of damage but there were none. Not even much dust had been dislodged. His conclusion was that most of the force had been directed into the floor. Mostly things blow up, not down. He was left scratching his head, declaring it was an unexplained incident and that angels must have been looking after us. He could find no cause of the mishap.

Afterwards my daughter, Aurora, was telling one of her friends about the accident. A couple of weeks earlier, her friend had seen the flash of a picture in her mind. It was of an explosion in a factory. She was busy around the house caring for a toddler at the time and just quickly asked God to send His angels to deflect the blast downward into the ground. Was it a coincidence? I doubt it.

The ambulance officers were due to go off duty, so they were very pleased when I requested to go to our local hospital. No such luck. They informed us that the hospital could not adequately treat my injuries, and we began the long trek into the city. So much for being home in time for lunch! During the trip, one of the medics helped me dial my wife's number so I could tell her what had happened. I tried to keep my voice calm, but shock completely undermined my efforts. I figured it was still better than hearing it from someone else.

The rest of the day was a blur of waiting, x-rays, drips, doctors and morphine. The pain, held at bay by shock, had hit me like a freight train and I was grateful for the injection that softened the edges.

Sarah came. It was so good to see her familiar face. Afterwards she told me, tongue in cheek, that she didn't mind me having the morphine at all. She reckoned it made me all lovey-dovey and gooey and that maybe I should try it a bit more often.

My thumb was dislocated, with the tendon completely severed. My radius was a mess in five pieces. Amazingly, no damage had been done to the major nerves or blood vessels running within a whisker of the shards. Again, the word miracle was mentioned more than once.

The medicos were more concerned about my belly, which by now looked like nothing I had ever seen before. The bruising was spectacular. They prodded and poked.

"Does this hurt?"

"No."

"What about this?"

"No, no, no!"

"And this?"

"No! It's just my hand! Look at my hand will you please?"

Finally, they sent me home with a half plaster cast, painkillers, instructions to keep my arm elevated, and an appointment for surgery at, yet, another Sydney hospital on Friday.

The day of my surgery finally dawned. Sarah drove the unfamiliar roads through congested Sydney traffic to the hospital. It was sometime after midday that I was wheeled up to theatre.

By the time I returned from recovery, the waiting room had emptied of relatives and friends. All the people who had had surgery that day were gone and only Sarah and one staff member remained. It was late. The surgery had been much more involved than anticipated. Metal hardware now held my wrist in place beneath a sheath of bandages and a slab of fresh plaster cast.

Thirty minutes later I was on my way home. Sarah carefully navigated the city roads. Peak hour had begun to wane, but she struggled with driving the unfamiliar roads in the dark. Long stretches of roadwork with poor markings and uneven surface increased the difficulty.

It wasn't long before I was feeling every corrugation. The pain medication was wearing off. We stopped long enough for me to take the two little pain killers I had been given, but they did nothing to stop the escalating agony. We were passing a turn off to a hospital, but I just wanted to go home. Even the freeway seemed bumpy, going on forever.

By the time we reached our hometown, it was no longer in question. I was in shock, almost passing out from the excruciating pain. I had no arguments when my wife drove me straight to casualty in our little country hospital where I was met by the same nurse who had greeted me on my first visit less than a week earlier.

What followed was a long night of morphine alternating with agony.

Long before dawn, Sarah picked me up again for the return trip. Only the team who had done the work could authorize the removal of the half plaster cast that had grown too tight around my swollen wrist. The long trip back was made more bearable by yet another injection.

We arrived to discover that nobody could see me until the hand clinic opened at 9am. That was two and a half hours away!

I sat on a chair outside the hand clinic, with Sarah standing in front of me

CALEB

holding up my arm. There was no choice but to wait in the deserted corridor until the hand clinic opened.

By the time 9am came, several others had joined the wait. The doors opened, and we slowly made our way into the clinic. One man seemed determined to be first in line. Sarah stepped forward as soon as he had been seen.

"You were not next." The male nurse did not glance up from his paperwork.

"Excuse me! My husband was operated on in this hospital just yesterday afternoon. He has spent the night in casualty in agony, and he is in shock with the pain. You will see him!" She did not raise her voice, but there was no mistaking her determination. His head snapped up to look around the room. The sight of me, pale and shaking, finally galvanized him into action.

I was taken to another room where I was poked and prodded some more, given yet more morphine and, after consultation with the surgical team, the plaster was removed, and finally, some measure of relief. The pain was still intense but no longer unbearable. Amazingly no damage had been done by the constriction. After some time, the half plaster cast was replaced, and I was told I could go home.

Sarah had other ideas. She explained to the staff, politely but firmly, how far we had to travel and that if this happened again, we had no morphine at home. She can be determined when she needs to be. My normally compliant wife had reached her limit.

A bed was found for me, and by late afternoon, Sarah began the journey home, exhausted and alone. She had to stop at a fuel station to sleep for a bit because she felt herself dozing off on the freeway.

I was discharged later the next day.

∼

In the space of less than a heartbeat, my whole world had been blown apart. The one area I excelled in—being practical, capable, a craftsman—had shattered to pieces.

That is who I am! Or was… I am not academic. I am good with my hands! *Was I ever going to regain the use of my right hand?* Sarah had to do everything for me, and I mean—everything. I couldn't let myself think about it too much.

During the next week, lying on the lounge with my arm awkwardly wedged between the back cushions to keep it elevated, I spoke to Emmanuel about it. He didn't say all that much, but he showed me a picture of a new hand in a gold box lined with blue velvet. There was no flash of light or instant transformation, but it gave me hope. I knew, somehow, that I would be okay.

So began six months of trips up and down the highway to the city for physiotherapy and doctors' appointments. We saw the physiotherapist who specialized in hand injuries, three times a week to begin with, and there were hourly, painful exercises every day in between.

Jade, the physio could be ruthless as she pushed my reluctant digits into position. "If you don't put them there, they will never go there," she said as she made me yelp in pain yet again. I was struggling to get my pointer finger and my thumb to even meet!

She knew her stuff, telling me horror stories of people who lost the use of their hand through not faithfully doing the exercises she was prescribing. Not me. I was going to do those torturous, difficult little movements just like she told me. Absolutely! The miracle was not going to happen in a flash, but in one tiny painful movement at a time.

It was very much the 'one block at a time' and 'discipline being my friend' thing that Emmanuel had talked about. I knew he was with me, helping me every single, painful day. The relationship I enjoyed in the Roller, so close but also somehow sporadic and intermittent, was becoming just as real in my everyday life.

Touching my pinkie with my thumb for the first time, squeezing a cube of foam, I celebrated each little triumph as slowly, ever so slowly, I regained the use of my right hand. Small victories added up until, after six months, I had full use of my hand. My thumb doesn't quite bend back as far as it did before, but hey! I could lift and bang and make and do, anything I could do before, and all without pain. Yes, it was a miracle!

Chapter Twenty One

To celebrate my recovery and our February wedding anniversary, we packed up the new camper trailer and headed to Tasmania for a well-deserved holiday. Boy, did it feel good. Sarah and I relished our time together, aware that we had been given a second chance. I could have so easily lost the use of my hand, or even my life, in the accident. Gratefulness seemed to intensify the colours and beauty as we treasured the moments. 'Tassie' is breathtaking with sensory overload at every turn. Even her brutal, colonial history, so confronting to contemplate, fed thankfulness.

On our return, feeling well rested and revived, I found myself able to, once again, face the unfinished renovation.

I tackled the outdoor area that had stumped me previously. I built timber steps and laid eighteen hundred pavers to create a large barbeque and entertaining space—all with my right hand! The drainage worked out perfectly. We also completed gardening and concreting projects.

It was not long after we returned from our trip that Jason, my brother-in-law, rang me. Jason and Anna had been concerned for me. They had been very aware of the difficult time we had faced, and they had supported us both. Our girls, as well as many other family members, had been incredibly caring.

"Hey mate. How about I come down and give you a hand? You haven't got much more to do. I will come, and we can break the back of this thing. Okay?"

I readily agreed.

He is a builder, and he knew exactly what to do. He braced inside the roof where the roofline changed direction to form an L shape. He used long pieces of timber to hold everything in place. He showed me what to do with other problem areas. He did it easily, unfazed by things that had stumped me.

"This place, it has always moved since the day it was built, and it always will. It won't be very much anymore. You may get some tiny cracks, maybe not. You have done a great job." His encouragement meant so much. His practical help put the capstone on the work. I could not find words to express my appreciation.

In a surprisingly short space of time, the remaining jobs were completed, about five years from when we had started. It had taken years longer than what I had anticipated, but as I stood back and surveyed the completed project, I could honestly say that it was good. The house was beautiful, inside and out.

Overcoming the inbuilt flaws of the house and the movement caused by the insidious ground water had taken more than I ever would have expected. There had been many setbacks, and there were some things I could never get right, some things I had to accept as they were, imperfect, but still good. I still struggled with discouragement, at times, but never again would I experience the completely mind stunning numbness I did that time when we returned from our holiday to see those cracks in the recently painted walls and render.

I had returned to the Roller on many occasions since my hand incident just to hang out with Emmanuel. After the house was completed, I wondered if, maybe, it was time to continue our journey. When I had asked Emmanuel about it earlier, he had seemed completely relaxed and said that this was where we needed to be for now. *I don't think he is in any hurry.* It was what I needed, with everything that was going on in my life.

I had driven around the perimeter of the large park-like field searching for an exit but hadn't found one. That hadn't made sense because I figured that the people who were already there must have gotten there somehow. I had said hello to them but hadn't felt inclined to reach out any further.

Now that my hand had healed and the house was finished, I decided to raise the question again with Emmanuel.

"There is one more thing before we head out," was his enigmatic reply.

"Okay. Let's do it." I wanted to continue, get on with the journey I had come to appreciate so much. I wanted to reach the city I had seen in the distance.

It looked like roadkill, like an animal mown down by a road train, mangled and bloodied. This is a common sight, especially out west during drought. Animals come to feed on the verges of the road where moisture condenses overnight and sustains small amounts of grass. Kangaroos have no road sense and are easily mown down by the enormous road trains. Smaller vehicles inflict less devastation, but they are nonetheless deadly to wandering wildlife, even close to our cities and towns.

Although it looked just as crushed, this one was not lying beside a lonely outback road. It was suspended in mid-air, on some sort of contraption. I moved closer so I could see.

CALEB

Wait! It's human! A man, arms spreadeagled!

Wait—wait… aaargh! Harsh sobs escaped my constricted throat.

Spasms gripped my body at the horror I was witnessing. Pain and grief erupted, exploding in my brain.

It's Emmanuel! He's dead! Nobody could survive that.

"No—No—NOOOO!" My cry sounded disembodied, anguished.

I sank to my knees, trembling like a reed in the wind. *My friend— Emmanuel—please—no—no…* I couldn't take my eyes off the sight. I wanted to look away, to hide, but I could not.

A slight movement—a shuddering breath—startled me. *He's still alive! How?*

My attention galvanized onto his face. *Could it be?* Slowly, deliberately he turned his head towards me, and one painfully swollen, bloodshot eye caught mine. His eyes, always his eyes, had captured me.

Emmanuel!

My whole being convulsed in deep-seated sobs. Grief overwhelmed me and I became unaware of time. As I held his gaze, snippets of memories, of conversations, my thoughts, my heart, played like a film reel across my mind.

Harsh, intolerant blame and judgements I held against myself exploded from the depths of me, allowing my scrutiny. I became aware of critical words and belittling thoughts, of self-loathing that were ingrained patterns in my life. The weight of it crushed me and I sank down to my hands and knees, no longer able to hold his gaze. It was as if a piercing light was penetrating my soul, exposing its filthy nakedness. *Could I accept myself too? Could I forgive myself?*

Somehow, I knew it was what I needed to do: to forgive myself. If I had been hard on others, I had been even harder on myself. I had put 'you should' on myself, constantly, obsessively. I had blamed others for doing that, but I had done it to myself! I had punished myself, even whipped myself, so very severely.

He had helped me forgive my Dad, my Mum, the clown, and others, but now—could he help me now?

"Help…me…please."

"Caleb." he said my name, in a raspy whisper.

Just one word but somehow it gave me the strength I needed to look up again.

He did this for me—for me…

As I looked into his badly swollen, battered face, forgiveness and acceptance cascaded over me in waves. He knew the filth that I harboured, the lowest, most shameful parts of me. He knew all along and he still loved me.

He had forgiven me, accepted me, completely.

Somehow, I could forgive myself. The crushing weight I felt began to lift. It was as if my warehouse, that had been so dingy and dark, crowded with dust-covered junk, was being completely transformed, swept clean and new. Now it was being filled with order and light.

I stayed, lying face down, for a long time, just letting it happen.

Occasionally, a ragged sob escaped my throat, and my body trembled for long moments as if I had a high fever.

Slowly, stillness came, peace seeping into every crevice of my body and soul. My mind, no longer tortured by shame, could rest.

I slept.

I awoke slowly, the gory sight still etched on my brain. I kept my eyes closed as I remembered. Gradually, awareness returned, and I became conscious of my surroundings. I was no longer lying prone in the dirt. I was curled up like a baby. I could feel soft leather against my cheek, and I knew that I was once more in the Rolls Royce, lying on the backseat.

I inhaled the smell of the leather, familiar and comforting. Memories of what we had done together, what he had done for me, chased through my consciousness. There was so much. Through both excruciatingly difficult and delightful times, he had been with me. The peace that had permeated my being like liquid gold was still there, warm and reassuring.

I refused to open my eyes. I didn't want to face being in the Roller without Emmanuel.

Emmanuel, my friend, my restorer; could it really be that he was gone? My chest felt hollow at the thought. I wondered at the incongruity. *How could that feeling coexist with such wonderful peace? To feel both empty and full, simultaneously—how could that be?*

A sigh escaped me, involuntarily. To attempt to understand all that had happened was too hard—it was bigger than me. Maybe I could look at it in time, but not now, not yet.

"Caleb." His familiar voice spoke my name. My eyes snapped open. I could hear his smile before I saw it.

"I'm not dead. I'm alive."

Epilogue

This journey has never been about getting the house right or conquering trading. It was always the foundations of my life that were the issue. They had never been laid down properly—not ever.

So, what has this journey, this difficult, challenging journey done for me?

I am no longer lurching from one crisis to the next. I have discovered that whether I'm moving forward, making progress, or ground to a stop and stuck—I'm okay.

Even when the worst happened, even when I couldn't use my right hand and didn't know if I ever would, somehow…

Whether I am understood or completely misjudged, I am who I am. There are some things I will never be, but it doesn't matter. Amazingly, incredibly I'm still okay.

Life is not perfect, but it is good, it is very good.

So much has changed, but the biggest is that now I can embrace myself, accept myself; a flawed human being, a man on a journey, a man who lives in two worlds. There is bedrock to my life now that was never there before.

And most importantly—I am never alone—not ever. Emmanuel is with me.

So much love, so much kindness—always. He was so different to how I thought he would be; so incredibly kind to me.

Always, he has seen me, every step of this journey, accepted me—broken, damaged—but he saw me. He has never put me down or mocked me, not once.

I am so very grateful to my friend, Emmanuel. So very, very grateful.

∼

"Dad is no longer the same man we grew up with."
Aurora

Glossary

4x4 A four wheel drive vehicle.

Aussie	An Australian (pronounced as if spelt with 'zz').
Bloke	A man.
Chooks	Chickens.
Chuffed	Happy.
Cooee	A call to get someones attention.
Cop, copping	Taking a hit, an unexpected blow, emotionally or physically.
Darn	An expresion of annoyance.
Dings	Indents or damage.
Dogs	in share trading, shares that loose a lot of value, also referred to in the book as puppies.
Doozy	Extra large, unusual or unprecedented.
Dud	Something that doesn't work, worthless.
Esky	Icebox or cooler.
Fair dinkum	something or someone is genuine, also an expression of annoyance.
Fizzy drink	Carbonated drink, soda.
Flippers	slang for people who renovate for the purpose of making money.

Flippin' heck	A softer alternative to swearing.
Fobbing off	To persuade someone to accept someting of lower standard, being pushed aside, or disregarded.
Gotta	Got to.
Guys	Men.
Having a lend	Joking at someone's expense.
In sync	Synchronised.
Knocked up	Out of breathe, exhausted.
Mate	friend (or a useful term when you forget someone's name).
Muck up	Behave badly, ruin something, play.
Newbies	Someone who is new at a job or task.
Nuh	No.
Physio	Physiotherapist.
Reno	Short for renovation.
Road kill	Animals killed on ther road.
Roller	Rolls Royce.
Snowies	The Snowy Mountains of NSW.
Stuff up	Make a mistake.
Stunned mullet	Dazed and uncomprehending.
Swag	A portable sleeping unit.
Tassie	Tasmania.

Tin Lizzie   Slang for A Model T Ford.

Ute Short for utility vehicle.

Vegies   Vegetables.

Yeh Yes.

If you recognise Caleb in yourself or someone else, please use 'kind' glasses to view them. As you discover the changes in Caleb's attitudes and perspectives unfolding in the pages of this book, know that the same person who helped him can also help you.

If you would like more information about the Immanuel approach, you can visit Dr Karl Lehman's website at
www.immanuelapproach.com
Then go to Getting Started

CALEB

www.ingramcontent.com/pod-product-compliance
Lightning Source LLC
Chambersburg PA
CBHW070253010526
44107CB00056B/2446